PSYCHIC EMPATH

Survival Guide for Empaths, Become a Healer Instead of Absorbing Negative Energies. Development, Telepathy, Healing Mediumship, Mindfulness, Meditation, Aura reading and Chakras

© **Spiritual Awakening Academy**

TABLE OF CONTENTS

Introduction 6

Chapter 1: Understanding Psychic Empaths 10

    What is an Empath? 10

    History of Psychic Empaths 12

    How Empaths Feel 14

    Common Traits of an Empath 14

        Highly sensitive 15

        They have good luck 16

        They hate conflict 16

        High sensory stimulation 16

        Their instincts about people are on the money 17

        They have imaginary friends 17

        They appear lonely 17

        They have a past life 18

        Communicate with animals 18

        Loving and compassionate 18

        Sleep issues 19

        Good at connecting dots 19

        They have trouble letting go 19

        Soak up other peoples' energies 20

        Highly intuitive 20

        Overwhelmed by relationships 21

        Take long to process emotions 21

        Love nature 22

- Strong senses 22
- Components of Empathy 27
  - Getting Others 27
  - Creating Others 27
  - Utilizing Diversity 27
  - Political Awareness 28
- **Chapter 2: Understanding Psychic Empaths** 29
  - How Empaths Feel 30
  - How Empaths Obtain Information 31
- **Chapter 3: Empaths and Spiritual Hypersensitivity** .. 33
  - How to Cope With Spiritual Hypersensitivity 34
  - **There are also several spiritual healing tools that you can use:** 35
    - Prayer 35
    - *Water* 36
    - *Mindfulness* 37
  - Essential Oils 37
    - Lavender 38
    - Rose 38
    - Chamomile 39
    - Frankincense 39
  - How to Use Essential Oils for Hypersensitivity 40
    - Aromatherapy 40
    - Oral Application 40
    - Topical Application 41

Chapter 4: The Benefits of Developing Your Intuition and Psychic Abilities 42

    The sensation of pressure disappears 42

    The connection with the spirits 43

    Learning and spirituality 43

    Heightened sensitivity of your physical senses 44

    Intuition 44

    Miles away from negativity 45

    The desire to eat healthier food 45

    Making new friends 46

Chapter 5: The Psychology behind Empaths 47

    The Shamanic and Mystical Understanding of Being an Empath 49

    How to Find Peace Living as an Empath 54

    Essential Oil Recipes for Anxiety 56

        Lavender Neck Rub 57

        Calming Essential Oil 57

        Anxiety Blend #1 58

        Anxiety Blend #2 59

        Anxiety Blend #3 60

Chapter 6: The Difference Between Empaths and Highly Sensitive People 62

Chapter 7: Signs You May Already Have Psychic Abilities .. 67

    Why do People Ignore their Psychic Abilities? 67

    Signs that you have Psychic Skills: 68

Chapter 8: How to Develop Your Psychic Abilities for a Better Life 78

Chapter 9: Exercises to Boost Your Psychic Abilities 86

Chapter 10: Parenting Empath Children — Tips for Raising an Empath Child 88

    How to support sensitive children 91

    The future of enlightened parenting 107

Chapter 11: Clairvoyant Healing 109

Chapter 12: Telepathy 117

Chapter 13: Aura and Aura reading 124

    What are Auras 124

Chapter 14: Mediumship 130

Chapter 15: How to Boost Your Psychic Abilities 136

Chapter 16: How to Embrace Being an Empath 142

    How to Become an Assertive Empath 146

    Learning How to Set Boundaries 149

    How to Become an Extroverted Empath 152

Chapter 17: Common Myths That Psychic Empaths Should Never Believe 156

Conclusion 167

Introduction

In psychology, empathy is a key component of being emotionally intelligent. In a world that is starting to appreciate emotional intelligence over the more traditional intelligence that is book smart, empathy counts as the main ingredient for improved social interactions. Empathy is defined in dictionaries and by psychologists as: the ability to understand and share in the thoughts and emotions of another person. In other terms, empathy entails putting yourself in another person's shoes so that you can understand where they are coming from and how they feel. It involves seeing the world from the perspective of another person so that you can appreciate their world, fears, struggles, and even joys much better.

Empathy is not the same thing as sympathy, even though most people will use the two terms interchangeably to refer to the same thing. While sympathy is mainly just pity, empathy involves going the extra step of trying to find a solution for someone's suffering. Sympathy says, "Oh, that's terrible, I feel so sorry for her" and then walks away, while empathy stays a bit longer in hopes that they can alleviate the pain at hand. Most human beings are born with the capacity to be empathetic. However, the extent to which this capacity is explored depends on the kind of nurturing that a person receives as they grow up.

So far, empathy does sound like a good thing. In fact, the world would be a better place if all of us were empathetic towards each other. There would be less judgment and less resentment. The world would be friendlier and a safe place where people's feelings and thoughts would be given equal priority, and nobody would feel unseen or unheard. Unfortunately, we do not live in an idealistic world where everything is perfect and flawless. We live among people who are capable of empathy, and also among others who consider empathy a weak concept. There is still another category of people who are completely incapable of being empathetic.

In our day to day lives, we demonstrate the ability to be empathetic towards others when we set aside time and energy to commiserate with their suffering. Even when we are best-intentioned, there are instances when we might not act in ways that are empathetic towards others. Other times, we might only feel some sympathy and then move along. This brings us to a slightly different category of people who demonstrate a more advanced form of empathy. These people are known as empaths.

An empath differs from an empathetic person in this way: while empathetic people are able to relate with other people's thoughts and emotions, empaths actually feel these emotions and thoughts as though they were their own. An empathetic person might relate to the pain of a colleague and then go on with their life. An empath will usually wallow in this pain because they feel it as if it is their own. A psychic empath is able to pick up another person's pain without necessarily being told. Their psychic ability allows them to tune into the suffering of another person even when this may not be so obvious to those who rely on verbal and visual cues.

There are different reasons why some people are empaths, while others only seem to experience moments when they are empathetic towards others. Nature is the first culprit in churning empaths. Some people are born with heightened sensitivity. You can see it in the way they respond to things, even when they are still small babies. They seem more alert and more attuned to their surroundings. The kind of nurturing that a person receives while they are growing up can also impact their development into an adult empath. If your sensitivity is honored for the gift that it is, you will likely grow up in the full glory of your empath self. On the other hand, experiencing trauma as a child has been shown to hinder a person's empathic abilities. Think of it this way —a child that is brought up in a caring and loving household has a better chance of becoming a caring and loving adult when she grows up.

If you are a psychic empath, you might have a very hard time going through the day since you are constantly surrounded by all this pain and suffering that you are aware of. It is important to learn how to shield yourself from emotional, mental, and physical drain while at the same time helping those who need your help. However, you must learn how to tell the difference between those who genuinely need your help and those who are only trying to take advantage of you.

In this book, you will learn everything you need to know to go from being a psychic empath to being a psychic empath *warrior*. A psychic empath warrior is one who harnesses their power to do good, instead of simply being at the mercy of their abilities and the energy of those around them. As a psychic warrior, you will have greater control over your emotions, and you will not go through life feeling overwhelmed and drained. You will learn to recognize the qualities that set you apart from the average person, how to identify energy vampires, and how to protect yourself from situations that will drain your energy. If you have always struggled to understand why you feel things the way you do, this book will act as a handbook that will make everything clearer.

The main objective of this book is to help you realize that what you have is a great gift that you can use to positively impacting the world and others while also taking good care of yourself.

Chapter 1: Understanding Psychic Empaths

What is an Empath?

An empath is a person with the special gift of perceiving the emotions and feelings of other people as though they were their own without even trying. They are naturally tuned in to the energies floating around them. If an empath walks into a room and sits next to a person who's quietly mourning, the empath will pick up on the sorrow and experience it as though it were their own. An empath who lacks awareness of their gift can be deeply conflicted, as they cannot tell apart their own feelings from those of others.

Ask yourself the following questions to find out if you're an empath:

- Can you perceive people in some way?

- Do you feel people's emotions and mistake them as yours?

- Can you think along the same line as other people?

- Do your feelings change as soon as you meet a particular person?

- Do you sometimes wonder whether you're co-dependent, neurotic, or even crazy?

- Can you read peoples' minds?

It can be awesome having the ability to pick up on other people's energies, but on the downside, it can be a real struggle when the said energies are of the dark nature and especially if the empath in question knows nothing of their ability.

Empaths are born, not made. Their abilities are genetic traits, inherent in their DNAs and are often passed through generations. This means being an empath is not something that you can learn. It's either you're an empath or not at all.

Being an empath means you're always open to process the energy and feelings of other people.

Empaths tend to openly feel and become more conscious about what is outside than what is within them. This can make empaths disregard their own particular needs. Empath are generally non-aggressive and non-violent individuals. Most of the time, they act as the peacemaker. Any place or situation filled with chaos or disharmony creates an awkward, uncomfortable feeling in empaths.

In case they find themselves caught in the middle of an argument, they will strive to fix the issue as fast as possible, or avoid it altogether if they can. If any foul words or profane language is expressed in their defense, an empath is likely to resent his lack of discipline and self-control.

Empaths have great interest in a wide variety of music to match their numerous expressive temperaments. Others can be puzzled at how empaths can listen to one music genre and switch to something completely different within minutes. Empaths pay close attention to the lyrics of songs. Words have powerful, adverse effects on them, especially if the song is relevant to their current situation or recent experience. In such cases, it is advisable for an empath to listen to music with no accompanying lyrics to avoid creating havoc in their emotional state.

History of Psychic Empaths

Since prehistoric times, psychics played a notable role in human culture. They often held positions as priests, priestesses, seers and mystics in various religions prior to the inception of Christianity.

Many psychic seers can be found in the Bible, including Samuel, Gad and Amos. Samuel was the one who found the donkey of King Saul. Gad was King David's personal seer, while Amos was the seer commanded by Amaziah to escape Judah and practice his prophetic endeavors outside that land.

One of the most recognized names in ancient psychics is the Greek Oracle of Delphi. The Oracle wasn't a single person, but rather an office held by the cleverest woman in Delphi. She interpreted information directly from Apollo, the God of Light and Truth. Her visions were increased by the natural steams emanating from the hot springs in the Delphi area. In ancient Egypt, the well-known seers were the priests of Ra on Memphis. In Assyria, oracles were called *nabu*, meaning "announce" or "to call."

During the Renaissance period in France, Nostradamus became a famous name in prophesying. His prophesies are still well-recognized across the globe and have been on print consistently since they were first written.

In mid-1800s, when the planet Neptune was discovered (a planet that rules psychic energy), the Spiritualist Movement began and expanded. Many psychics flourished during that period, including Edgar Cayce, Daniel Dunglas Home, and Madame Blavatsky.

Psychic empaths have walked the Earth ever since the dawning of humankind's history. However, it was only during the New Age Awakening of the 1970's and 80's that empathic skills were recognized as being distinct from other psychics.

How Empaths Feel

Since empaths are highly sensitive to the different energies surrounding them, they often fall victim to inner conflict and tremendous stress. When an empath's empathetic nature is in full effect, he may experience abnormal nervousness or feel as if an electrical current is suddenly overpowering him. This is followed by an overflow of emotions.

Strong melancholic feelings may arise out of nowhere and engulf him. This can become confusing for the empath since he may not completely understand what's happening to him. He takes on those feelings as his and tries to formulate an explanation as to why he feels such unfounded emotions.

Because of this, it is no surprise that most empaths become terribly depressed at some point of their life. Depression may even be a recurring visitor for many of them. Besides negative emotions, empaths can also absorb other people's positive vibrations. However, this up-and-down phenomenon can create an emotional rollercoaster ride for the untrained, unaware and inexperienced empath.

Common Traits of an Empath

As an empath, these are some traits that you're bound to display:

Highly sensitive

People keep on telling you that you're too sensitive. This is because what they say or do can affect you quite easily. You can read into their unsaid messages when they talk or do something. This sensitivity can make you susceptible to things that don't hurt well-adjusted people. Your high sensitivity makes you give a lot of thought to what you do or say. This pattern always leads to self-inhibiting tendencies. You end up customizing yourself too much so that the world can fall in love with you. The habit of suppressing your true emotions comes with a cocktail of challenges.

Telepathic

Psychic empaths can transmit thought patterns from their minds to another person. Also, they can know the thoughts of other people no matter the distance between them. For instance, a psychic empath will instinctually know when either of their parents is sad or depressed, as they can share in the sadness deep within. A psychic empath could be eating ice cream one moment, and the next moment they sense something is wrong, and when they contact someone about whatever they have thought, it is normally the case.

They have good luck

A psychic empath seems to be followed by good luck. They not only bring luck on themselves but also on other people. For instance, if a psychic empath meets with someone and exchanges greetings, that person will proceed to run into good luck throughout the day. If a psychic empath gives someone some money, chances are the person will run into more good fortune for the better part of that day or week.

They hate conflict

The easiest way to make a psychic empath run away from you is to confront them or issue a threat. They love making peace – not warring. They are extremely turned off by the idea of having to fight as a way of righting a wrong.

High sensory stimulation

The sensory nerves of a psychic empath are very active. For this reason, they tend to react to stimuli much quicker than the average person. A psychic empath can get overwhelmed too easily. For this reason, they tend to avoid places with too much noise or too much light – anything on the extreme end. Psychic empaths are also good at detecting sensations that would be lost on the average person. They can detect subtlest things about a place or person.

Their instincts about people are on the money

Psychic empaths know by gut what someone is like. For this reason, if you're a bad person, you won't catch a psychic empath entirely off guard. They will know that you're a bad influence but somehow still give you the benefit of the doubt, and after you reveal your true colors, it will dawn on them that their first instincts were accurate.

They have imaginary friends

A psychic empath is in contact with the spiritual world. They have even made friends with entities in the spiritual realm otherwise known as spirit guides. The spirit guides act as protectors for the psychic empath and reveal secrets and insights to them. Strangely enough, the psychic empath may derive more satisfaction from interacting with spirit guides than they ever would from interacting with regular people.

They appear lonely

To the average observer, a psychic empath can be the loneliest person for they are always alone. However, psychic empaths hardly ever seem needy or emotionally unstable. They may lack human contact, but that doesn't automatically mean that they are lonely. They tend to have very active imaginations. The worlds that they have created in their minds are extremely fun-filled. But then again, there is a percentage of psychic empaths that crave human contact and are lonely.

They have a past life

Psychic empaths are old souls who have existed someplace else before. Oddly enough, they have a faint recall of their past lives. A psychic empath will think back to their past life, and though the memory is not vivid, they have a somewhat basic understanding of what life was like in that world.

Communicate with animals

A psychic empath seems to have the uncanny ability to communicate with animals. Maybe they will establish eye contact or touch the animal, and then the information starts flowing. Animals are completely at ease around psychic empaths

Loving and compassionate

Psychic empaths don't stay away from people because they think they are superior to them; they stay away because people overwhelm them. This doesn't mean that psychic empaths are incapable of expressing love. They express warmth and compassion to the people whom they have close ties with. The best part is that this is genuine compassion. Psychic empaths cannot possibly fake their love.

Sleep issues

Psychic empaths battle an array of sleep-related problems. Their sleep problems probably began in early childhood. The issues may range from bed-wetting, nightmares, and even insomnia that have had a negative effect on their quality of life.

Good at connecting dots

Psychic empaths are extremely creative, and they can piece together disjointed parts to form a whole. Their ability to connect dots enables them to find solutions to existential problems. If they develop their creative potential, they can end up becoming innovators or great artists. Many psychic empaths tend to obsess about connecting these dots so that when one piece is complete, they quickly start connecting the next set of dots.

They have trouble letting go

Psychic empaths don't open their hearts at everyone trying to catch their interest. However, once they open their hearts, they tend to love with a ferocious will. For this reason, terminating a relationship with a psychic empath would be disastrous. They have trouble letting go after investing much of their emotions into the relationship.

Soak up other peoples' energies

You could be having a fantastic day with your spirits high, and then you go to Starbucks and sit next to a family who unbeknownst to you just lost one of their members. Nothing is said. All are sipping at their coffee with quiet faces. Ever so slowly, the joy you first had begins to fade away, and in its place, sadness takes over. You have no reason to be sad, but you experience this sadness anyway. Soon, the family gets up, leaves Starbucks, and then your sadness fades away. You had just absorbed their energies.

Introverted

Being introverted is not the same as being shy. A shy person might loathe being alone and feel rejected for lack of human contact, but on the other hand, an introvert gets drained when they stay too long with other people, and they cherish being alone. A shy person has self-inhibiting tendencies, but an introvert has a strong sense of self and stays true to it. Empaths are more likely to be introverted than extroverted. They don't shun all human contact but prefer socializing on one-on-one terms, or within small groups.

Highly intuitive

One of the most effective weapons in an empath's hands is their gut feeling. They have this ability to sniff out the true nature of a situation. This makes it a bit hard to play games with an empath. They will see right through your tricks. As an empath, if you meet someone, you tend to have a gut feeling of what that person is really like. You are always in tune with your surroundings and can tell when there's danger. This ability is one of the main advantages of being an empath because you're less likely to be taken advantage of.

Overwhelmed by relationships

Conventional relationships put emphasis on partners spending as much time together as possible. An empath cannot thrive in this kind of arrangement because they constantly pick up on their partner's emotions and mistake them as their own. This is not to say that empaths cannot form any relationships. However, the traditional arrangement of a relationship needs to be deconstructed. For instance, they can have a room of their own that they may retreat to when their urge to be alone kicks in, and also, their partners should be patient with them.

Take long to process emotions

The average person has a laser attention to their emotions. Whether sadness or joy, it kicks in suddenly. Their emotional reflexes are fast too. An empath takes the time to understand the emotions that they are currently feeling. For instance, if something terrible happens, the sadness won't register immediately. They will first try to process the situation, going over the details time and again, and then the sadness will well up inside them. They can experience emotions in such a powerful way. Thus, whether it's sadness or joy, they feel it to the full.

Love nature

For most empaths, they are at their happiest when surrounded by nature. Whether it's the sunlight kissing their skin, the rain falling on them, or taking in a gulp of fresh air; no other activity restores their balance as being surrounded by the natural world. They feel a deep sense of connection with nature. When an empath is experiencing a tsunami of emotions, one of the restorative measures would be taking a stroll through an open area beneath the sky.

Strong senses

An empath boasts of very developed senses. They can catch the slightest whiff of an odor, can see into the shadows, can hear the tiniest sound, and can feel the vibrations of various other things. These developed senses make them so good at noticing the small stuff. Empaths notice what would ordinarily escape the attention of most people. For this reason, they tend to flourish in careers that demand close attention and the exploration of the abstract.

Generous

There isn't a more selfless person than an empath. They don't have to have something to help. They are willing to go the extra mile and be of help. For instance, when an empath comes across a street child and sees their suffering, it tugs at their heart. They not only want to give them some food but also find a way of removing them from the streets. The majority of the world doesn't care about street children and see them as an annoyance. We can assume that the empaths of the world play a critical role in helping street children and other people who are experiencing hardship.

Creative

Empaths tend to be very creative. This is aided by the wealth of emotions that they are always experiencing. Their creative nature manifests itself in almost every aspect of their life — food, relationships, homes, and most importantly, career. An empath is likely to do well in a career in the arts. They have tremendous potential when it comes to drawing, writing, singing, or making films. They tend to portray their emotions unambiguously and can capture the emotions of other people just as intended.

- Empath Categories
- *Geomantic empaths*: These empaths are attuned to a certain environment or landscape.

Geomantic empaths are connected to specific sites like buildings, lakes, oceans, and mountains. These empaths can feel the historical emotions of these sites. For instance, if an empath visits a site where people were slaughtered many years, they can still feel the sorrow. Empaths attach feelings to different environments so that each environment evokes certain emotions. Such empaths tend to carry souvenirs to remind them of various environments.

- *Physical empaths*: Also known as a medical empath, they can pick up on the condition of someone else's body. They would instinctively know what ails another person. In extreme cases, they can pick up on the symptoms so that they share in the pain of the other person. Physical empaths also have healing abilities. They tend to take careers in conventional or alternative medicine. Physical empaths are great at taking care of ailing people. Those who have ailments trust them instinctively because they can feel that they care.

- *Emotional empaths*: They are sensitive to the emotional energy floating around them. As an emotional empath, you will absorb the emotions of other people and think that they are yours. This can be deeply distressing if you're constantly around negative people. An emotional empath should increase their self-awareness so that they can tell apart their emotions from those of others. Emotional empaths tend to withdraw from other people so that they can spend time alone and recharge. An emotional empath should protect their energy by following various healing practices.

- *Animal empaths*: You have certainly seen someone in your neighborhood more interested in keeping company with animals than human beings. They have a certain pet or even various pets that mean the world to them. There's a high likelihood that such a person is an animal empath. An animal empath feels a deep connection toward animals. They can sense what the animals want or feel and the animals love them back. The connection is so deep that they have a way of communicating with each other. An animal empath answers to their intense desire of connecting with animals by domesticating their animals of choice. Also, they tend to be passionate about animal rights and make contributions to funds that advance animal welfare.

- *Plant empaths*: A plant empath shares a deep connection with a certain plant or plants in general. The plant evokes certain emotions when they touch it. A plant empath can communicate with the plant and can know its condition. They like hanging out near the plant in a natural environment, bringing it into their house, or planting it in the garden.

- *Precognitive empaths*: Are you the type of person that can always tell the future? And this is not down to your future alone, but also the future of other unrelated people or events? You're certainly a precognitive empath. You tend to "see" things before they come to pass. Your visions are made manifest in various ways such as dreams or feelings. Having this ability to foresee the future is both rewarding and distressing. It can help you brace for the future, and at the same time, it can amplify your misery knowing the pain that awaits you.

- *Psychometric empaths*: This sort of empath has a deep connection to various physical objects. The physical objects arouse certain emotions in them. The objects could range from utensils, knives, jewelry, photos, etc., but they each awaken certain deep emotions when the person comes across them. For instance, if your dad handed down his knife to you and then died that same day, the knife could have a lot of sentimental value. Every time you come across such a knife, you would miss your dad terribly.

- *Telepathic empath*: A telepathic empath can know what is stored away in someone's mind. With a casual glance at that person, they can tell their unexpressed thoughts. This causes the empath to have too much insight into people and situations.

Components of Empathy

Getting Others

Tune into enthusiastic signals. Listen well and focus on nonverbal correspondence, grabbing inconspicuous signals subliminally. Show affectability, and comprehend others' viewpoints. You can help other individuals when you comprehend those individuals' needs and sentiments.

Creating Others

Creating others means following up on their needs and concerns and helping them to create to their maximum capacity. Individuals with aptitudes here for the most part reward and commend others for their qualities and achievements, and give productive input intended to concentrate on the most proficient method to improve.

Utilizing Diversity

Utilizing decent variety means having the option to make and create openings through various types of individuals, perceiving and commending that we as a whole carry something else to the table. Utilizing decent variety doesn't imply that you treat everybody in the very same manner, yet that you tailor the manner in which you cooperate with others to meet with their requirements and emotions.

Individuals with this expertise regard and relate well to everybody, paying little respect to their experience. When in doubt, they consider decent variety to be a chance, understanding that different groups work much superior to groups that are increasingly homogeneous. Individuals who are great at utilizing assorted variety likewise challenge narrow mindedness, inclination and stereotyping when they see it.

Political Awareness

Numerous individuals see 'political' aptitudes as manipulative, yet in its best sense, 'political' signifies detecting and reacting to a gathering's enthusiastic propensities and power connections. Political mindfulness can assist people with navigating authoritative connections successfully, enabling them to accomplish where others may beforehand have failed.

Chapter 2: Understanding Psychic Empaths

There are different kinds of empaths who specialize in specific types of psychic work. Geomancy is a skill in which the empath senses the energies and vibrations of the earth. You can use this skill in dousing, detecting water underground, or predicting upcoming bad weather. Psychometry is the psychic ability, which enables an empath to obtain impressions from various objects. This is sometimes used by the police in solving strange or violent crimes.

Clair cognizance is another unique skill in which the empath knows exactly what measures to take or actions to perform in any given situation, especially during an emergency or a crisis. They can act with self-assurance, peace and calmness, inspiring everyone around them to act in the same way.

Some empaths can also sense spirits and work with them, a psychic ability called mediumship. Some can heal by feeling other people's symptoms and help them by transmuting energies. Similarly, they can help others overcome emotional traumas. Some empaths can communicate with nature in general while others do the same with animals. Precognition is another rare gift in which psychic empaths can perceive events or disasters that are about to occur.

While empaths are endowed with significant abilities as mentioned above, they often pay a high price for these. Often, they are being judged and misunderstood. Sometimes, they also receive derogative, even contemptuous, remarks for their declarations. Empaths can be particularly sensitive of their environment, causing them to acquire physical up-sets and strange allergies that cannot be diagnosed by regular medical practitioners.

Although their talents and abilities are truly significant, they are not all-knowing. Their skills may not work at optimum levels all the time, nor can they heal all ills and diseases of mankind.

How Empaths Feel

Since empaths are highly sensitive to the different energies surrounding them, they often fall victim to inner conflict and tremendous stress. When an empath's empathetic nature is in full effect, he may experience abnormal nervousness or feel as if an electrical current is suddenly overpowering him. This is followed by an overflow of emotions.

Strong melancholic feelings may arise out of nowhere and engulf him. This can become confusing for the empath since he may not completely understand what's happening to him. He takes on those feelings as his own and tries to formulate an explanation as to why he feels such unfounded emotions.

Because of this, it is no surprise that most empaths become terribly depressed at some point of their life. Depression may even be a recurring visitor for many of them. Besides negative emotions, empaths can also absorb other people's positive vibrations. However, this up-and-down phenomenon can create an emotional rollercoaster ride for the untrained, unaware and inexperienced empath.

How Empaths Obtain Information

The true mechanisms of psychic/empathic abilities are still unknown. Numerous theories have been made in an attempt to explain such mechanisms, but all of it were mere matters of conjecture. Not all empaths possess only one ability. Some can obtain information using multiple psychic skills that work in unison to create one "mega" psychic ability.

For instance, an empath may use his psychometric abilities to obtain information by simply touching a person or an object. Then, his empathic ability processes that information to induce feelings. Looking beyond those two psychic abilities, the empath may also possess strong clairaudience, clairvoyance, and other skills that facilitate the processing of all the information he is receiving.

It can be difficult for a psychic empath to find ways to control the information he receives until he stops to evaluate his individual processes and determine if he is operating only on empathic abilities or a set of abilities. Testing oneself on each potential ability requires a great deal of patience and time. However, once the empath has successfully established a baseline, it will be much easier to comprehend how his individual psychic ability is related and how his combined abilities function and interact.

Chapter 3: Empaths and Spiritual Hypersensitivity

Empaths often suffer from spiritual based hypersensitivity; the symptoms include:

- Your environment causes you to feel overwhelmed

- Sounds are too loud, even if made at a normal range

- You constantly feel the feelings of others

This type of energetic overwhelm is nothing new; the spiritual community has been dealing with it for many years. As more and more empaths choose to ignore their gift, they are becoming less connected with the universe, which has led to an increase in spiritual based hypersensitivity. Oversensitivity to people's energy and noise is a common reaction to energy acceleration, as you ascend to higher heights in your spiritual development, you should expect to experience this. When you begin to accelerate in the spiritual realm, you may feel like a radio signal picking up a million signals at once. When there is a shift in spiritual vibration, your sense of intuition and your emphatic channels are open causing a heightened awareness of the thoughts and feelings of those around you. Spiritual hypersensitivity can manifest physically causing third eye dizziness, hypersensitivity to energy, odors, light and noise.

Metaphysics believes that the body is a vehicle for the spirit, the body is not who we are; our person is carried in our spirit. Wayne Dyer states that we are spiritual beings living in a physical world. Everything that happens in the physical first happens in the realm of the spirit; therefore, if there is an imbalance in your spirit it will manifest through your physical body. Metaphysical wellness counselors always address the spiritual aspects of healing before focusing on the physical, and it is spiritual alignment that cures the physical ailments.

How to Cope With Spiritual Hypersensitivity

When the body is overwhelmed physically, emotionally or mentally, the fight or flight syndrome is activated and breathing becomes shallow. When you begin to experience a change in your breathing pattern, you should immediately start practicing conscious breathing. This is where you focus your attention on your breath, which will slow down your nervous system and allow you to relax. Breathe slowly, deeply and in a rhythm at the same time as focusing your mind on being able to relax in the situation that you are in. You should always take a temporary retreat from any stressful situation such as family or work-related conflicts. Excusing yourself to the bathroom is a good way to do this. This will allow you to get away from the negative energy, practice your breathing techniques and renew yourself.

There are also several spiritual healing tools that you can use:

Prayer

Depending on what you believe in, prayer can always bring comfort in an overwhelming situation. One of the most talked about and effective prayers is the H'oponopono prayer.

So how can you heal yourself with H'oponopono? There are four steps to the concept:

- *Repent:* Say you are sorry for the part that you have played in the things you perceive as evil or problematic that are surrounding you. As an empath you can say that you are sorry for the pain that the people you have met recently are experiencing. Whatever you feel responsible for, say you are sorry for it; feel the remorse and mean it.

- *Ask for Forgiveness:* You are probably wondering, "Well, who am I asking?" We all have our different belief systems. The majority of us and especially empaths believe in some kind of higher power and so that is who you ask to forgive you.

- *Gratitude:* Say thank you; there is so much power in gratitude. If you take your focus off the negative, you will find that you have so many things to be thankful for. Say thank you that you woke up this morning. Say thank you that you have eyes to see, a nose to smell, legs to walk on, that your internal organs are all in working order. Find something to say thank you for and say it continuously.

- *Love:* Love is the most powerful force in the universe; saying the words, "I love you" over and over again will bring love into your life. You can say I love you to your cat, your house, your car, the sky, the trees! Whatever you feel love towards, say it.

Water

Water has extraordinary balancing and healing properties during times of hypersensitivity. When consumed with consciousness, it provides inner alignment. You can balance the surrounding energy by putting a drop of water on your third eye area. When you apply water that you have energized, it leads to even more powerful results. You can energize water by praying over it, or putting a word on the bottle with the intention of infusing the words frequency into the bottle. Words such as healing, calmness, and peace work well.

Mindfulness

This technique can pull calming energy into the body. Focus on your breath at the same time as looking at something beautiful like a rose, the sun or the sky. You can even focus on the palm of your hands as if this is the first time you have seen them. You can redirect the attention you are paying to your feelings by focusing on something visual.

Essential Oils

Essential oils have a calming effect and can greatly improve the anxiety associated with spiritual hypersensitivity. The American College of Healthcare Sciences conducted a study in 2014, in which 58 hospice patients were given a daily hand massage for one week using a blend of essential oils. The oil blend was made up of lavender, frankincense and bergamot. All patients reported less depression and pain as a result of the essential oil massages. The study concluded that essential oil blend aromatherapy massages were more effective for depression and pain management than massage alone.

The following are some of the best oils for treating anxiety:

Lavender

Lavender oil has a relaxing and calming effect; it restores the nervous system, provides inner peace, better sleep, causes a reduction in restlessness, panic attacks, irritability and general nervous tension. There have been several clinical studies proving that inhaling lavender causes an immediate reduction in anxiety and stress. One study discovered that taking lavender oil capsules orally led to an decrease in heart rate variation in comparison to the placebo while watching a film that caused anxiety. The study concluded that lavender had an anxiolytic effect, which means that it has the ability to inhibit anxiety.

Other studies have concluded that lavender has the ability to reduce anxiety in patients having coronary artery bypass surgery and in patients who are afraid of the dentist.

Rose

Rose alleviates depression, anxiety, grieving, shock and panic attacks. The Iranian Red Crescent Medical Journal published a study in which a group of women experiencing their first pregnancy inhaled rose oil for 10 minutes at the same time as having a footbath. A second group of women experiencing pregnancy for the first time was also given the footbath but without the rose oil inhalation. The results discovered that a footbath combined with aromatherapy caused a reduction in anxiety in nulliparous (a woman that has not had any children yet) women in the active phase.

Chamomile

Chamomile oil is known for its calming effect and its ability to produce inner peace, reduce worry, anxiety, over-thinking and irritability. The University of Pennsylvania School of Medicine conducted an explorative study and found that it contains medicinal anti-depressant properties. The National Center for Complementary and Integrative Health also found that chamomile capsules have the ability to reduce anxiety related symptoms.

Frankincense

Frankincense oil is great for treating anxiety and depression due to its tranquil energy and calming effects. It also helps you focus, quiet the mind and deepen meditation. A Keimyung University study in Korea found that a combination of lavender, frankincense and bergamot reduced pain and depression in hospice patients suffering from terminal cancer.

How to Use Essential Oils for Hypersensitivity

Essential oils are either ingested, applied topically or used in aromatherapy. Here are some suggestions for their usage:

Aromatherapy

Aromatherapy is a very popular remedy for anxiety because of the human ability to process information through smell; it can trigger a very powerful emotional response. There is a region in the brain called the limbic system that controls memory recall and emotional processing. Inhaling the scent of essential oils stimulates a mental response in the brain's limbic system, which regulates stress and calming responses such as the production of hormones, blood pressure and breathing patterns. You can use the oils in the bath, a hot water vapor, direct inhalation, a humidifier or vaporizer, cologne, perfume, a vent or aromatherapy diffusers.

Oral Application

You can consume the majority of essential oils orally. However, it is essential that the oils you use are safe and pure. The majority of commercialized oils have been blended with synthetics or diluted with other substances making them unsafe for ingesting. The most effective method for consuming essential oils is to combine a drop of oil with a teaspoon of honey or drop the oil into a glass of water. You can also add a couple of drops to the food you are cooking. You can place a couple of drops under your tongue. This is particularly beneficial because the blood capillaries are located under the tongue near the surface of the tissue, which allows the oil to quickly absorb into the bloodstream and travel to the area of the body where it is required. You can also take essential oils in capsule form.

Topical Application

Topical application is the process of placing essential oils on the skin, nails, teeth, hair or mucous membranes of the body. The oils are quickly absorbed by the skin. Due to the strength of the oils, it is essential that you dilute or blend them with a carrier oil such as coconut, avocado, jojoba, or sweet almond oil. You can apply the blended mixture directly to the affected area, around the rims of the ears, the soles of the feet, in the bath, through a warm compress, or through a massage.

Chapter 4: The Benefits of Developing Your Intuition and Psychic Abilities

If life is a resume, then psychic abilities can be considered valuable points in it. Even so, it's not their existence that makes them important, but the fact that you can help other people by using them. It is like having a beautiful horse, one of a kind, but savage, that can't be ridden. That horse becomes truly special when you succeed in domesticating it and start using it for your purposes.

Thus, having and developing your psychic abilities and your intuition can have numerous advantages and benefits as listed below.

The sensation of pressure disappears

If you learn how to develop your "third eye," situated between your eyebrows, you will be able to pick up energetic signals, and your chakras (each of the seven centers of spiritual power in the human body) will open up. This way, you will instantly lose the pressure and be more relaxed. It is the same with going to a spa where they rub your forehead and you can relax and let go of your stress and problems. The fact that evil is a part of our world, doesn't mean that all the energies are negative. By absorbing only the good energy, you motivate your brain to think of positive thoughts and eliminate the pressure within.

The connection with the spirits

Your stronger connection with the spiritual world helps you develop your mediumship. Besides the fact that you can maintain a connection with your deceased loved ones, you will also be able to help other people connect with theirs. Even a person with no psychic skills can stay in touch with his or her "angels." You, of course, never want your family members and close friends to die, but that is the order of things. Connecting with spirits is a good alternative for those who can't let go of their relationships with their late loved ones and still want to maintain them. Sometimes this is not okay, considering the spirits were once humans too and don't like to be bothered at any hour. So, nevertheless, you need to respect them.

Learning and spirituality

After you have your psychic awakening, you will want to learn more about this world. As you open up, you want to read and know as much as possible and walk a more spiritual path. The good news is that there are plenty of learning resources that you can use. Thousands of articles and magazines deal with this subject and people all over the world have written stories about their psychic experiences, paranormal traditions in each country, mystic rituals, and ways to become a better psychic and person.

Heightened sensitivity of your physical senses

If you realize that your hearing is heightened and your vision is clearer, it means that your physical senses are getting stronger. It is all about meditation. The more you let go of the material world, the better you see the world around you and realize what is really important to you. Finding peace with your inner self is a rule for having a better and more balanced life. Your senses will never lie to you, so if you feel that they're accurate, it is clear that your mentality is changing in a good way.

Intuition

It might be a little frightening to have the sensation that something is about to happen, but a developed intuition is a perfectly normal thing. Even Albert Einstein believed in intuition. It is a known fact that women have sharper intuition than men. The explanation comes from the fact that ladies pay more attention to details, are more sensitive, and have tighter relationships with their loved ones. Their sensorial fields detect the negative energies more easily. Animals have highly developed intuition too, especially the ones crawling (lizards, snakes), as well as rodents. A female rat senses a calamity, an earthquake or a flood, way before it happens, so she has time to move her babies to a safe place. So, in the end, intuition is useful in helping you foresee the bad and avoid it, when possible.

Miles away from negativity

You may find that you can easily pick up on the emotions of people around you, but there is nothing bad about being empathic. In fact, nowadays empathy and common decency are the values that we need the most, the lack of which causes us stress and other physical problems. Also, because your sensitivity is heightened, you might feel drained in the presence of some people. Usually, these people are charged with negative energy, so try to stay away from them as much as possible.

Finding your psychic abilities and helping them develop within you is like a morning hike in the mountains. You start the journey feeling like you can do it, you climb higher and higher, and you don't feel your energy drained, but continuously rising, and in the end you arrive at the mountain top. You look back at the road you just finished and you are surprised at your own strength. You knew you had it in you, but you never thought you'd get here.

The desire to eat healthier food

Once you go through long meditation hours and yoga breathing classes, you will decide it is time for you to start having a healthier lifestyle altogether. The alimentation is, of course, part of it. Just as you decided to eliminate the negative energies from your body and mind, you decide it's time for your stomach to be cleansed and filled up with things that are good for you. Vegetables and fruits are always a good idea, but no matter what you choose to eat during your diet, try to keep a balance between the physical and psychical elements.

Making new friends

Throughout this entire period, your soul will grow and you might realize that some of your old friends have remained at the same non-developed level as before. You will feel sad for leaving them behind, but it's the best thing you can do if you don't want them to drag you down. The only thing you can do is and pray for their own good. After that, you can start imagining the new friends the Universe has in store for you. Hopefully, they will be people with the same abilities as you and will understand and motivate you to develop as a psychic more and more.

Chapter 5: The Psychology behind Empaths

Empaths are typically lacking something in their lives, such as attention, love, sense of belonging, and/or affection; thus, they want others to have what they are lacking in hopes of getting it in return. Even the most depressed and drained empaths will do whatever necessary to help lift up others.

Science also plays a role. Dr. Judith Orloff (2017) explains that there are five scientific explanations that give more insight into empathy.

- The mirror neuron system
- Electromagnetic fields
- Emotional contagion
- Increased dopamine sensitivity
- Synesthesia

The mirror neuron system. It has been found that there are cells in the brain that are directly responsible for compassion. Mirror neurons enable empaths to mirror others' emotions and feelings. For instance, if someone is sad, empaths will be sad as well. On the other hand, narcissists, sociopaths, and psychopaths are said to be empathy-deficient. They basically lack the ability to have empathy for anyone. These individuals are like this because their mirror neuron system is underactive. Mirror neurons are typically triggered by an event that occurs to someone else. Those who lack mirror neurons will not feel any emotions for us if we are sad, hurt, or happy.

Electromagnetic fields. Another scientific finding that has been found is that the heart and brain create electromagnetic fields with the body. The fields are transmitters of people's emotions and thoughts. Empaths can be sensitive to this input, and it will cause them to become overwhelmed and anxious over it. The sun and earth also have an effect on emotional responses.

Emotional contagion. When we are able to feel everyone else's emotions and feelings around us, we need to pay attention to the people we hang around with. Do not spend time with people who drag down your positive energy. As an empath, it is extremely easy to feel as others do. For instance, it is said that someone has empathy if they catch someone else's yawn. That is considered an emotional contagion. When one person yawns, many others will do the same. Most people have some sort of contagion sense, such as if a baby cries, the rest of the babies in the nursery cry as well. The ability to catch other people's moods is very important when it comes to relationships and understanding how the other might be feeling at any given time. In order for empaths to block out everyone's bad emotions, surround yourself with those who uplift you instead.

Increased dopamine sensitivity. Dopamine is what causes people to react with a pleasure response. Introverted empaths actually need less dopamine to feel happy, hence why they enjoy being alone. Dopamine sensitivity is usually found more so in introverts, while extroverts need to have higher levels of it in order to feel happy. Extroverts actually love the stimulation from going to parties, and they crave the dopamine rush.

Synesthesia. Those who see colors when they listen to music have synesthesia. This is considered a neurological condition where there are two senses that are paired together in the brain. This is also called mirror-touch synesthesia, in which people can feel the emotions in their bodies as if they were theirs.

Empathy will get us through many situations and will allow us to respect others even if we disagree with them. It is good to have an open heart, but watch out for those who will try to take advantage of you.

The Shamanic and Mystical Understanding of Being an Empath

Shamanism and mysticism are two completely different practices. They have different values, either that of empowerment or surrender. Whether or not you are drawn to one or the other will be the deciding factor of what spiritual needs, desires, or interests you are looking to fulfill.

Shamanic

Let's first learn what the shamanic point of view is. The belief is that all of humanity is connected to one another, and this is considered the collective unconscious. The shamanic way is to feel empowered. Empaths tend to follow the shamanic path as they are able to connect to anything around them at any given time. Empaths have the gift of connection, the gift that allows us to feel connected to people around us. In early May of 2004, Mystic Familiar took part in a worldwide medicine wheel meditation. This included an actual shamanic medicine wheel that spread across 600 miles of Northwestern United States. The purpose of the medicine wheel was to help relieve people of negative energies from ourselves and others around us. The goal is to be reactive in the connectivity to others.

Shamanic practices are ways to heal the earth, heal oneself or others, channeling and mediumship, as well as entering a state of trance for wisdom. This is done to heal a connection to a higher power or a spiritual entity. This can be done with stones, plants, sounds and songs, flowers, herbs, and crystals.

There are many signs that you might be a shaman, but the top five consist of the following:

1. Your ancestors were healers as well.
2. You have a strong connection with nature.
3. You do not fit in with others.
4. You are able to "read" people.
5. You feel as though you are called upon to help and heal others.

Your ancestors were healers as well. Chances are, if any of your ancestors were healers, you may also have that gift. There are cultures that believe that this gift is passed down from generation to generation.

You have a strong connection with nature. Shaman recognizes that everything is interconnected with one another. The relationship between us and nature is seen as mutually dependent as it nurtures us and we nurture it. We need one another in order to survive, so it is best to nurture both.

You do not fit in with others. Most cultures have seen shamans as outsiders or different. Shamans have unique gifts and sensitivities, and because of that, they do not fit into a typical society. They do act as a bridge between the higher world and those on this level, and they are respected for the knowledge and wisdom that they share. Shamans focus on empowerment and have a way to help guide their lives as well as the lives of others.

You are able to "read" people. When you "read" people, it means that you can tell what their character is just by looking at them in the eye. You can also tell if they are battling an illness or a spiritual issue that they must overcome.

You feel as though you are called upon to help and heal others. A shaman does not like to see suffering. When they do, they have a very strong urge to heal it. They want to reestablish what harmony was lost during the time of suffering and want all aspects to connect together in peace. The desire to help, heal, and assist others in regaining peace and harmony in their lives is at the forefront of any shaman's mind. If they can help, they will.

Mystic

The top five signs that you may be a mystic include the following:

1. You are not materialistic.
2. You do not need to follow the norms of society.
3. You prefer to be alone.
4. You can see right through people.

5. You are not afraid of the future.

You are not materialistic. You do not believe in wasting money on material items, such as brand-name clothing, fancy cars, big homes, or the most recent electronics. You basically think that people who parade around with materialistic items are showing how shallow they can be.

You do not need to follow the norms of society. You do not need any validation in order to be who you are. You seek validation from within yourself and do not follow along with anyone just to fit in.

You prefer to be alone. You are always seeking a higher understanding of life and those around you. You enjoy your alone time as it allows you to reflect on what is going on within you as well as around you.

You can see right through people. If you are just meeting and conversing with someone for the first time, they may embellish stories about themselves. You will recognize that right away and will withdraw from being around those types.

You are not afraid of the future. Mystic individuals tend to see change as an opportunity to grow and obtain new opportunities. They do not fear the future; they embrace the changes that occur and keep moving forward.

Mystics tend to believe in attaining an insight into human mysteries. They generally believe that we are interconnected with nature and understand the preservation of all around us in order for each to survive. If one portion of the connection is broken, all the others that are connected will suffer.

How to Find Peace Living as an Empath

Being an empath can be exhausting and draining, so you need to find a way that works for you that will help you regain your peace. There are a few ways to help with this, such as the following:

1. Centering
2. Grounding
3. Shielding

Centering. This is a great way to release stress from stimulation. It is important to become aware of your physical and energy bodies and focus on maintaining that awareness. This is the first step toward spells, meditation, and praying. It will help make you aware of what emotional items belong to you and what do not.

Grounding. A way to think of grounding is to become one with the earth. Even if you are using the floor in a building, you will still be able to release or regain energies. The most important thing is to get as low to the floor or ground as you can. Some sit Indian-style on the floor of their office in order to ground themselves. It is important to know that there are different ways that people ground themselves in order to maintain peace for themselves. Some people sit on the floor and hold on to a stone. They focus on how the stone feels to relax their minds and help meditate to release energy and regain their peace.

Shielding. In order to block out unwanted energies, it is best to shield them so you are not overwhelmed with numerous energies. Most experienced empath use a shield that is called semipermeable. With these types of shields, you are not completely closed off, but at the same time, you are not constantly taking in energy in either. When you become experienced with shielding, you will find that you are able to function more efficiently due to more positive energy.

Centering, grounding, and shielding are ways to manipulate your own energy and turn it into something positive. These are all related to one another and can be performed together or separately. "Empathy is a psychic/energetic phenomenon, and psychic/energetic solutions are one of the most direct ways to manage it". The practices may be difficult to learn at first; however, they are worth it in the end to maintain your own peace.

Essential Oil Recipes for Anxiety

Anxiety is a real deal for many empaths, and it can become so overwhelming that there have to be many options to try to decrease the anxiety level or keep it at bay. "While the actual results of essentials oils like doTERRA and Young Living and their ability to cure most common ailments is widely debated, it doesn't stop people from incorporating these oils into their daily life". First, let's see which oils are best to combat anxiety:

1. Lavender
2. Rose
3. Chamomile
4. Ylang-ylang
5. Frankincense

Surely, there are more, but those seem to be the most popular that everyone has heard of. Just the scents alone may help combat your anxiety, but if you are having a large bout of it, it is best to try some combinations.

Here are the top five essential oil recipes for anxiety:

Lavender Neck Rub

One of the most popular recipes is the lavender neck rub.

Ingredients:

- 3 drops of pure lavender
- 1 teaspoon fractionated coconut oil or almond oil

Directions:

1. Blend the lavender and coconut or almond oil in a small bowl.
2. Spread the combination on your neck for instant relief of anxiety.
3. You can use this during the day when you find yourself getting stressed or consistently before bed.

Calming Essential Oil

This recipe can be used to alleviate all anxiety symptoms. It can be used as perfume. You can put it in a vial with a rollerball top and rub it on your skin, or it can be put in a diffuser.

Ingredients:

- 2 drops germanium

- 2 drops clary sage
- 1 drop patchouli
- 1 drop ylang-ylang

Directions:

1. You have to personalize the application to your own preferences, such as whether or not it will be in a rollerball applicator or through a diffuser. If you are using the rollerball method, add 30 drops of the combination into a 10 ml vial, then rub it on your wrists, feet, and neck in order to alleviate anxiety.

2. If you prefer to use this combination through the diffuser, just add the blend to the diffuser pad, and you will sense the aroma to calm down. This is best used before bed or if you prefer on the go when you feel your anxiety getting to heightened levels.

Anxiety Blend #1

This recipe will tame anyone's anxiety when it shows its ugly head. Once you get this going, take a couple of deep breaths, and you will be as calm as a cucumber.

Ingredients:

- 2 drops cedarwood oil

- 2 drops wild orange oil
- 1 drop ylang-ylang oil
- 1 drop patchouli oil

Directions:

1. Combine the ingredients in a small bowl and add to the diffuser pad. This blend works better in a diffuser so you can escape with the natural scent and defeat any anxiety you may have had. This is best administered 30 minutes to one hour prior to going to bed.

Anxiety Blend #2

This blend will soothe muscles throughout the body, creating an amazing sense of relaxation, alleviating any tension or anxiety.

Ingredients:

- 2 drops bergamot oil
- 2 drops clary sage oil
- 1 drop lavender oil

Directions:

1. Mix the ingredients together in a small bowl until they are fully blended. Place the combination in the diffuser as this blend is best

received via aromatherapy. Utilize as much as you need until you feel as calm and relaxed as you want to be.

Anxiety Blend #3

This is a natural wood-type aroma, so if you find that you are most relaxed when you are in nature, this would be the best for you to try.

Ingredients:

- 2 drops Roman chamomile oil
- 2 drops petitgrain oil
- 1 drop atlas cedarwood oil

Directions:

1. This blend is best in the diffuser, used as an aromatherapy. Combine the ingredients in a small bowl until they are fully blended together. This scent can be spread throughout the room in order to feel relaxed and calm. Another way you can utilize this is by placing your face over the bowl and breathing deeply until your level of calm is reached.

Essential oil recipes can be used in a few different ways, such as the diffuser, the rollerball perfume, or deep breathing over the bowl with the mixture. Each of these ways, with the combination of ingredients, will create an aroma-filled environment so you can bring your anxiety level down when you need it most. This may be combined when you are unwinding at the end of the day, reading your book, and deep breathing in the calming aroma. All in all, it cannot hurt to give this a try, especially when trying to maintain your anxiety levels from day-to-day emotions.

Chapter 6: The Difference Between Empaths and Highly Sensitive People

Though highly sensitive people and empaths almost seem to read from the same script, there are actually some differences between the two. What you must first understand is that being a highly sensitive person or an empath is not mutually exclusive. You can be both of them at the same time. The following are some differences between highly sensitive people and empaths:

Highly sensitive people take longer to wind down and restore their energy than empaths

Both empaths and highly sensitive people tend to get overstimulated after spending the day mixing with other people. While empaths recover from the overstimulation much quicker, highly sensitive people need much more time to recover from the overstimulation. For this reason, a highly sensitive person will seclude themselves much longer than the empath. Highly sensitive people, as the name suggests, tend to dwell too much on their sensory experiences. Their brains are wired in such peculiar ways to listen for certain keywords.

A highly sensitive person usually has a number of insecurities that make them incredibly self-conscious. It doesn't matter how perfect they seem to the average person, but once this insecurity creeps up on the said person, then it can be quite hard to overcome the insecurity. For instance, if someone grew up feeling ugly, they might internalize this feeling to the extent that no one will help them see themselves in a different light. When that person goes out and realizes people are giving them stares, they will automatically think that people are analyzing their looks and finding them ugly.

This will set off the alarm in their head about how ugly they are and what follows is a streak of obsessive thoughts. When a person is extremely sensitive, they tend to be sensitive about virtually everything. When they move from one concern, they will immediately find something else to stress about. On the other hand, empaths are sensitive, yes, but they are sensitive to the energies floating around them. This means that they stop feeling terrible once the source of their distress moves away from them. For this reason, after a day of mingling with people, empaths are in a far much better position to restore their energy than highly sensitive people.

Highly sensitive people are introverts whereas empaths can be either introverts or extroverts

For both highly sensitive people and empaths, the commonest personality spectrum that they share is that of introversion. Highly sensitive people are exclusively introverts whereas empaths – though a majority of them are introverts – could just as well be extroverted. To understand why a highly sensitive person has no chance of ever being an extrovert, you have to understand how their mind works. A highly sensitive person has beliefs in their mind that they keep looking for supporting evidence. Due to their extremely sensitive nature, they keep misreading what people meant. For instance, if a lecturer attends a session and keeps focusing his gaze on a certain highly sensitive girl, the girl might think that something is wrong with them, but unbeknownst to them, the lecturer actually finds them attractive to look at.

So, the girl will obsess about everything they think is wrong with them and this cycle of thought is absolutely draining. Ultimately, they will have to retire into some quiet place to regain their composure and energy. They cannot do without having to retreat into their caves – the classic introvert tendency. On the other hand, an empath plays the role of an emotional sponge. They tend to pick up on the vibrations of the people around them. If they are around good people, they feel good, and if they are around bad people, they start feeling bad themselves. This can also drive them to seek solitude. Except that there are empowered empaths who understand the condition that they struggle with.

An extroverted empath will choose to stay away from people who prey on their energy and associate with the good-natured ones instead. In other words, an extroverted empath will take advantage of their ability to soak up people's energies by choosing to soak up the positive energy.

Empaths can sense the subtlest energy

The ability of the highly sensitive people to pick up on subtle energies is not as fine-tuned as that of empaths. An empath can detect even the tiniest bit of emotion because they are connected to people on a very primal level. The empath seems to be able to access a person's mind and gain total access to their emotions. On the other hand, though a highly sensitive person would pick up on the energy of other people, they will merely pick up the general vibe and miss out on the subtlety. An empath is much more likely to go through the rollercoaster of emotions, but a highly sensitive person is stuck in a cycle of negative thoughts once triggered.

Empaths internalize the feelings of other people

When an empath perceives the emotions of other people, it doesn't stop there. They upgrade other people's emotions to become their own. Thus, if someone is in a world of pain, the empath is forced to feel the pain too. In that sense, the empath is at the mercy of the people that they interact with.

Highly sensitive people cannot internalize the feelings of other people. They have a million insecurities – real and imagined. What happens is that someone will say something or do something and the highly sensitive person will be triggered. Highly sensitive people have very sharp observation skills, and they vet people's deeds against their database of insecurities. Once the negative train of thoughts starts, there's no stopping.

Empaths have trouble distinguishing someone else's discomfort as their own

As an empath, you could be sitting in a lecture hall, trying to pay attention, and then *bam!* You start experiencing agonizing thoughts. Even though you have internalized those thoughts, you cannot tell the source. So, you just suffer quietly. On the other hand, the highly sensitive person can tell apart their emotional distress from those of others.

Chapter 7: Signs You May Already Have Psychic Abilities

Have you ever had the feeling that you already have some psychic skills or abilities? Perhaps you have plenty of experiences with déjàvu that you don't believe are significant, or you think that each time you accurately predict something, it's a mere coincidence. Are you guilty of ignoring unusual events that happen to you, or do you actually pause to look deeply? Many of us who already have psychic skills in one way or another do not recognize them for what they are, and so they go unused or worse, unnoticed. Recognizing the skills that you may already have is crucial for this path.

Why do People Ignore their Psychic Abilities?

Afraid to be seen as "Weird": Our world does not always glorify or praise higher seeing, which may lead some people to hold back their abilities out of fear of being seen as different or weird. People do not always appreciate it when others see more than they do, and may resent someone who sees deeply into reality and is open about it. When you don't have friends around who understand this interest of yours, it can be hard to listen to your intuition or stay faithful to your path.

Psychics are, at Times, seen as "Evil": At times, people with psychic abilities are even seen as witches, evil, or interested in the black arts, which is not necessarily true at all. As mentioned, everyone has these abilities, but most aren't aware of how to see them for what they are, haven't noticed them, or simply ignore them on purpose. However, some people may call these abilities evil, which will lead some to hide their skills. It's important to remember that these skills are not evil at all and are just a natural part of being a human.

It's also possible that the person with psychic abilities may be called crazy or nonsensical if they are open about their skills or use them in front of others. It's a shame that we live in a world that downplays such an important and natural gift, but being aware of some of the stigma against these abilities can help you move past being held back by it. Once you develop along your psychic path, these judgments from others will not matter to you as much.

Signs that you have Psychic Skills:

For someone who naturally has these abilities in a large amount, they can only be held back for so long before they come out. Read over some of these signs and symptoms that might mean you already have some of these abilities. Perhaps you will realize that you're already halfway there, and only need to know what you should be looking for. Once you are aware of what these skills look like, you can move onto developing them even further, or choosing which you want to focus on. Do any of these descriptions fit you?

Higher than Average Intuitive Abilities: Have you heard the phone ring and already knew who it was, before seeing their name on the caller ID? Perhaps you can sense it when a text message is about to be sent to you, or have known an event was coming before anyone else. If you have the ability to sense whether someone has good or bad energy from across the room, before even speaking with them, you have highly developed intuition. This is, as mentioned, the first step on the journey of uncovering all of your psychic abilities.

Visions Occur Regularly to you: For someone with psychic abilities, visions can be quite normal and occur often. If you've envisioned the future on multiple occasions, whether in dreams or waking life, you definitely have some level of psychic skill. These visions may depict what is happening in the hour, or the few months, and are significant at times, and seemingly trivial at others. In order to test this, start noting down your visions and ideas of what is going to happen, to see if you can confirm them on.

Déjàvu is Normal to you: Déjàvu is something that everyone has experienced at least once, but for someone with higher than average psychic abilities, it's a common occurrence. If you always feel as though you've seen this place before when you really haven't, or sense familiarity in new things, places, or people, you are probably going through déjàvu. This is a signal that your psychic abilities are already in tune. Once your psychic abilities are heightened even more, this might become an everyday occurrence for you.

Accurate Gut Feelings on a Regular Basis: For someone with psychic abilities, knowing what will happen before it does, is natural. You may be able to tell how events will play out, even if it's just a general sense of "good" or "bad". You may even be able to sense when you are going to get along well or badly with someone just from looking at them, or in extreme cases, sense when a natural disaster is about to hit across the world.

Occurrences of Telepathy: Have you ever felt as though your mind can send messages to other people? Have you picked up the thoughts or emotions of others seemingly without any effort? Perhaps you have noticed that you are having a connection with someone else without even saying one word, or have engaged in a full conversation with someone without talking at all. These are all signs of being psychic, and skills that can be strengthencd with effort and practice.

Vivid Dreaming: When someone has psychic skills, they often also have a tendency to experience vivid dreams, which they can recall even after waking up, in detail. They see symbols in these vivid dreams that can show deep metaphorical significance to the dreamer, and also show hidden messages that pertain to what is happening in their life at the time. A lot of people even have dreams that recur and tell a story that is hidden within the subconscious mind. Tapping into this skill can lend valuable insights to your own mind.

Sensing History of Objects or People: Being able to sense the history of an object or person after touching it or them is another psychic skill that you may naturally possess. One way in which psychics are so powerful is because they are able to sense facts about objects, places, or people by simply focusing. They sometimes are able to hug someone or hold their hand and suddenly experience or sense pieces of that person's past.

Premonitions and Predictions: If you've ever recorded thoughts down because you knew they were going to occur on, and then seen them happen, this is quite obviously proof of a latent psychic ability. You could have known they were coming from a dream you had, or simply a feeling that appeared to come out of nowhere.

You know when Trouble is Coming: There is a strong feeling that happens when someone senses their loved one in danger. This can cause you to panic for no apparent or immediate reason, and cause a huge impact on you. There might be no instant explanation for this feeling, other than the overwhelming sense that someone close to you is in trouble. In some cases, you might know who it is specifically, while for others, you will simply know it's someone close to you.

You feel Events from Far Away: This ability is quite advanced and tells you that you are definitely psychic. Perhaps once you were either at work or at home, and could sense something happening from far away, either in another city or even country. If you've felt experiences from across the globe and knew what was going on, right as it happened, you likely have very advanced psychic skills. This could have been anything from a detailed, clear vision, to a strong sense of trouble happening somewhere specific.

You have Healing Abilities: Some psychic people are able to touch someone ill or suffering and notice that they feel better almost instantly. Someone with psychic gifts has strong and usually positive energy that can be used to heal either mental or physical wounds in other people. If this has happened to you, it's likely the cause of your psychic abilities.

You Predict Future Events: This one is quite obvious, but being able to predict future events, telling them to someone close to you, then seeing the event actually occur, is one main way to tell that you have psychic abilities. These intuitions often come at the most unexpected of times, and often without rhyme or reason, until the event occurs and makes it clear for you.

Having Access to Sounds: Hearing sounds when no one else can, and always wondering why nobody is reacting to those subtle chimes or rings, can tell you that you have latent psychic skills. These noises might be pointing to an event that is yet to come. Some people with this skill are been able to narrow down what each sound means and use it to their advantage, or to help other people.

Possessing psychic abilities need not make you afraid or anxious. These skills are wonderful gifts and, when developed fully, can be used in extraordinary ways. Psychic people are very helpful and valuable to others that have yet to notice or harness their own skills in this arena. People tend to trust those with psychic abilities, even if they aren't sure why they trust them. This can be for multiple reasons, from guidance, to support, to solving mysteries, or even a simple intuitive pull. When you learn to embrace these skills as blessings from nature, you can begin to put them toward helping the world.

Psychics are a normal part of our society today. That's not saying there aren't people out there who do not believe in this sort of thing. Police departments have used psychics to help solve cold cases and abductions. Research has shown that psychics are real and are an accepted area of study. Studies have shown that psychic abilities are similar to the energy in quantum physics. Psychics can be seen on many TV shows as the main character. You can find many out there on this subject.

Religious leaders still disprove psychic abilities. They always warn their parishioners about the evils of psychics. They write them off as frauds, devil worshippers, or con artists. In spite of huge amounts of evidence that these abilities do exist, psychics still remain as unwanted guests in most religious institutions.

Psychic abilities go into more detailed information. It can help your intuition to build more from what you are feeling to make things clearer and give you better insight. This information can be brought through clairaudience, clairvoyance, clairsentience, clairgustance, or claircognizance. Instead of that gut feeling about not liking someone, you will either know something specific or see something specific about their past.

1. The first of the many intuitive abilities is clairaudience. This means clear hearing. You receive messages without using your actual ears. Clairaudience is inner hearing. You might have had someone tell you something, but no one is around you, or the person you are standing to didn't say anything. Psychics can hear spirits talk to them. It will be like you are reading to yourself. Sometimes, you might hear a voice in the accent of the person who is talking through them.

2. The second is clairvoyance. This means clear seeing. This is the most common intuition. Clairvoyance is being able to see something with your mind's eye. To simplify, it is like watching a movie in your head. This does not mean they are looking into the future or anything major; it is usually subtle. You could just see a number, color, or symbol. You will have to out what it means. It might actually be a premonition.

3. The third is clairsentience. This means clear feeling. This means you get messages through emotions, feelings, and sensations. Empathy is the most common form. People who are empaths usually feel drained since they are always bombarded by both negative and

positive emotions and feelings. You might walk up to someone you just barely know and can "feel" exactly what they are feeling. It gives you an ability to know if someone is lying. This is very handy. If your abilities are extremely strong, you might begin to feel sick when you are around a lot of people with bad energy.

4. The fourth is clairgustance. This means clear tasting. With this, you can taste something before ever putting it into your mouth. Mediums sometimes experience this during a reading. When psychics try to communicate with others, they might begin to develop a taste in their mouths. If the person they are trying to reach liked chocolate, they the psychic might actually taste chocolate.

5. The fifth is claircognizance. This is clear knowing. This ability allows you to know something without seeing any facts or information. You might just know that you can't trust your neighbor or that new person you just started working with. These feelings might be strong and just pop in your head at any time. You might have had some similar thoughts before. You might have been standing and waiting for an elevator, but something just told you to take the stairs.

When you get to the floor you wanted, you find out the elevator got stuck between floors.

A lesser common intuition is clairalience. This is clear smelling. This gives you the ability to smell beyond your normal ability. If you have ever been sitting, reading a, relaxing in your favorite chair and got a strong odor of a cigar, pipe, perfume, or any smell you can associate with a deceased relative.

These are just examples of different intuitions. You do not have to have all of them. You might only have one or two, or you could experience all of them at one point in your life. It all depends on how a person wants to communicate with you.

Chapter 8: How to Develop Your Psychic Abilities for a Better Life

Developing your psychic abilities can be a hard nut to crack if you have got no plans of how to do it. There are myriads of techniques that are of great importance in your journey of developing strong psychic abilities. With these techniques at hand, you might still find it very hard. The secret to this is that you have to practice only one technique per day. You do not necessarily have to practice these exercises in a given order as they all have one aim, that is, the development of your psychic abilities.

The following are the various ways in which you can develop your psychic abilities:

Take a walk in a park

Taking a walk in a park or any other place surrounded by nature is one of the best ways of meditating. This is where you get a chance to concentrate on your steps while walking. As you walk, keep focusing on each step you take while uttering the word 'step' after each step. This will help you a great deal in clearing the mind of confusion and jumbles.

Practice staring at auras

You can easily learn to always stare at an aura, and this is one of the best ways of developing your psychic abilities. The best way of coming up with an aura is having a friend standing in front of a wall with only one-colored paint. You are then required to step back approximately eight feet. Now you have to stare on his or her forehead while imagining that you are looking through her behind the wall. At this point, you will notice that there is an aura layer formed around their heads. This, therefore, will have greatly developed your psychic ability.

Pray often

Praying is one of the greatest tools for developing your psychic abilities. Prayer is a tool that many employ in relieving themselves of burdens as they talk to a Supreme being; they believe in. This also makes you feel supported and loved. Therefore, having some time designated for prayers daily will be of help to a great deal.

Make a symbol

There is a variety of ways in which you can obtain psychic information. They are usually not literal and thus have to look at symbolically. Everyone has got Spirit guides, and thus yours will guide you through the interpretation of information. You will, therefore, develop your psychic abilities in the process.

Make your tarot

In case you are using tarot to develop your psychic abilities, then you can get a tarot deck and make your tarot. Use your imaginations to make your meanings of the cards rather than looking at the meanings that come with them. You can also spend time with one card a day and meditate upon it the note down all you think about the card. This, therefore, will help you in developing your psychic abilities using a tarot.

Keep your vibration high

When developing your psychic abilities, it is imperative to have your vibrations high. This is because like is always attracted to like, and thus you will also be able to attract other souls that are spiritually aware. Apart from that, the frequency at which the spirits vibrate is very high.

Activities That Help in Psychic Progress

The more knowledge you have of people, the more able you are to pick up on messages from others. For example, if you are empathetic, you are able to place yourself into their situation and see things in a much clearer way. If you are inexperienced with different kinds of people, you are less likely to be able to read them or to give them accurate readings. Thus, there are some activities that you can do to help you to develop your psychic abilities:

Observation exercises – understanding body language

Observation is a wonderful tool. You are able to observe people and to see the different ways in which they react to certain situations. This gives you many clues when it comes to being able to assure them while giving them a reading or consultation. Body language is one way in which you can learn if people are being honest with you. It shows on their faces and the movement of muscles when someone is deliberately lying to you and as a psychic it's important that you know who you are dealing with. Try to learn from the body language of people and the best way to do this is to look out for the following things:

Crossed arms – This shows a defensive stance. The person may not be open to any new information and thus you must approach with caution.

Blinking eyes when they talk – This means that there is a level of deception involved. Perhaps the client is trying to show you up as a charlatan and is purposely feeding you incorrect information to see how you react to it.

Not looking directly into your eyes – This may mean that the client is a little ashamed of something and you may have to coax it from them in order to help the client. In this case, try to be gentle and reassure the client so that the client is prepared to confide in you.

Playing with their hands – This denotes that the client is nervous and it may help to sooth the client so that you are able to make him/her feel more at ease with you. Remember that trust plays a huge part when someone consults a psychic. You need to establish sufficient trust to take away any doubts that the client may have and help him/her to feel at ease.

Other behaviors to observe

If a client shows belligerence, the chances are that the client feels on unsafe ground. The reason that people show this type of behavior is that they feel a sense of insecurity. Perhaps they have never experienced psychic readings before and are a little ill at ease and use this bravado to hide the fact that they are insecure.

You also need to be able to recognize the following, in order to feel empathy for the client and this empathy is all important when it comes to making yourself believable:

- Nervousness
- Unhappiness
- Fear
- Anger
- Jealousy

- Hopelessness
- Loss of faith

These feelings could be derived from the situation in which the client finds him/herself and your empathy is very important. If, for example, a woman wants you to talk about her dead husband, it would be unprofessional not to pick up on her feelings of desperation or to exploit them. You need to be able to show empathy and to step into her shoes and if this means questioning her a little about the relationship, this will help your powers of observation.

Increasing your Knowledge

If you are lacking in general knowledge, you can't put yourself over as astutely as someone whose knowledge is vast. Thus, one of the activities that is suggested for people who want to develop their psychic abilities is reading. Read a wide variety of which will give you an insight into human behavior and even if you limit this to good quality fiction, this will help you to be able to empathize with clients who have been through experiences that you would otherwise not be able to imagine.

The wider your knowledge base, the better able you are to draw from it. I recommend that you choose a variety of – both factual and fiction – because reading opens your mind and helps you to experience all kinds of emotions that you may never touch upon in your life and that will be helpful to you in your work.

Concentration exercises

To develop and hone this part of your psychic ability, you need to have activities that improve your concentration levels. Art can do this if you are artistically inclined. If you like computers, why not try honing in on your concentrative powers by using something such as a program like Luminosity. You have to concentrate because you are given certain questions to answer within a given time. They call it "exercise for the brain" but as far as a psychic goes, it's really and truly great concentration for the mind. That's part and parcel of what you need to develop so if you can find programs that require total concentration, then these are good for you and will help your concentration levels to improve.

Other games that are fun are turning a pack of cards face downward onto a table and trying to establish pairs by turning two cards over at a time. You need to concentrate because you need to remember where certain cards are and, with practice, will find that you improve your concentration. This is vital for the psychic because it's easy to allow outside influence to get in the way when you are trying to give a client a reading. If you have learned concentration through meditation this helps to hone the mind, body and spirit into that moment. However, card games such as this also help your powers of observation and when working with people, that's vital to success.

Sociability – Learning to mix with all kinds of people opens up your understanding of different character types. It is important that you have a fair share of work and play and try to meet plenty of people in your life. Many people who develop psychic abilities find that having a great social life improves the way that they can read people's problems because they also become aware of different mannerisms and the approach that different people have toward their problems. It also helps to work with different age levels. Thus, spend quality time with kids and learn to have a great relationship with older folk.

Chapter 9: Exercises to Boost Your Psychic Abilities

It can be tricky to develop your psychic abilities, but these exercises can get your psychic senses and abilities rolling.

1. Meditate for at least 10 to 15 minutes every day to raise your energetic vibration and develop your psychic abilities.

2. Try guided mediation for variety and some fun.

3. Practice psychometry to see if you can sense, hear or see anything about the object and its owner. Hold a small metal object (ring, keys) that is used a lot in your hand and see if you can feel, hear and visualize the energy.

4. Use Zener cards with friends

5. Grab different types of flowers and study them for a little while. Next close your eyes and imagine the flowers to develop your psychic abilities, specifically, clairvoyance.

6. Walk outside your home and concentrate on each step as you walk. You can focus on the movement of your body and visualize the good things around you.

7. Read a few pages of a psychic development book every day.

8. Read about intuition and the spiritual world.

9. Spend time reading tarot cards as it is a great way to develop your psychic abilities.

10. Learn more about how chakras and auras work and practice seeing auras.

Chapter 10: Parenting Empath Children — Tips for Raising an Empath Child

Raising empath children may be difficult if we do not recognize the signs that they truly are an empath instead of just being difficult. Here are seven signs that may give you solidification that your child is an empath:

1. They are considered highly sensitive.
2. They are overwhelmed by stimulation.
3. They have a strong connection with animals.
4. They have an attachment to objects.
5. They love to read.
6. They have mysterious physical symptoms.
7. They enjoy their alone time and need a lot of it.

They are considered highly sensitive. There are many teachers and psychologists who may diagnose or proclaim that they are overly sensitive or too sensitive. Highly sensitive children may have sensory issues. Some may not like tags on their shirts and scratchy materials, and in some cases, detergents may cause rashes.

They are overwhelmed by stimulation. Have you ever been to a parade or a crowded theme park and there are children having meltdowns at the sight of so many people or loud noises? Those children may be experiencing an overwhelming amount of stimulation that they do not know how to handle. Strong scents, loud noises, and too many people around them may cause them to shut down with an anxious and overwhelming feeling that they do not know how to handle. For example, when the child screams and runs to the car when loud noises come up in the parade, do not laugh at that child. Try to find a way to comfort them so they do not feel so overwhelmed.

They have a strong connection with animals. Empath children tend to connect deeply with animals. There are not any facial expressions or odd body language to decipher, so they typically are on the same page with animals. There are not any conflicting expressions between the two. It is an upfront, non-judgmental relationship. Animals love their humans unconditionally, and the empath child will prefer their animals to other humans.

They have an attachment to objects. There are children who develop a strong attachment to inanimate objects. You may notice this when one of their toys breaks and has to be thrown away or their stuffed animal has a rip in the side. They tend to feel deeply for their toys and are attached to them, and they think that their toys feel pain and loneliness. Kids that have this attachment to their toys and stuffed animals are most likely empaths.

They love to read. On occasion, your child may become obsessed with a certain topic and will want to learn and read all about it. If your child falls in love with reading to escape into an alternate reality, all power to them, and do not discourage it.

They have mysterious physical symptoms. Physical symptoms will appear when a child bottles up intense emotions and is unable to figure out how to release them. In fourth grade, there was a child who was having a difficult time with her grandfather passing. She would carry around the stuffed animal that he gave to her, and she would have a hard time breathing on occasion and have chest pains. Doctors were unable to provide a diagnosis. They chalked it up to growing pains and anxiety. With the many emotions within the child, plus dealing with her surroundings at school, classmates, classwork, and such, she did not know how else to express how she was feeling. Hence, her internal symptoms developed into mysterious physical symptoms.

They enjoy their alone time and need a lot of it. As adult empaths need alone time, child empaths do too. Child empaths rarely get bored as they have solitude when they are alone and can entertain themselves.

They need this alone time to recharge or regain their solitude from certain situations.

Those parents that are empaths will generally pick up on whether or not one or more of their children is an empath as well. Many people, including teachers, parents, and counselors, tend to have a difficult time understanding children that are empaths. They do not quite understand the hypersensitivity and will think the child is dramatic or needs to be tougher like other children. They may want to help the child; however, they do not know how to, and at times, that can single out the empath child to the point where it may do more damage. It does not matter who understands them and who does not; all they need is someone to believe in them so that they can flourish into their own unique being.

How to support sensitive children

The Magic and Stress of Pregnancy and Infancy

What potential elements add to kids turning out to be empaths? Some may start as empaths in utero, ready to strongly feel everything, both cheerful and distressing. These kids are brought into the world with high sensitivities, rising up out of the belly incredibly receptive to outer boosts, much more so than different newborn children. In these occurrences, it appears that the empath quality is spent on genetically.2 Sometimes, however, this demeanor develops because of early childrearing. Parental job demonstrating is significant. Youngsters gain from their folks' empath traits.

Supporting an empath kid starts in pregnancy. Everything that occurs during this period influences the developing hatchling. Truth be told, regardless of whether a kid ends up being an empath, it's outstanding that babies are touchy to the enthusiastic condition of their folks. It has been appeared, for example, that some hatchlings appreciate Mozart however are upset by rap music.

Playing loosening up music during pregnancy can help quiet you and your child.

A mother's anxiety matters as well. Research has demonstrated that maternal pressure hormones cross the placenta and course in the hatchling, expanding a youngster's propensity to be "exceptionally strung."[5] When a mother encounters continuous clash with her accomplice or others, the baby gears itself up to arrangement with this sort of high-pressure condition and may then be inclined to different pressure related indications after birth.

The neurological wiring for affectability creates in the belly. It's critical to encompass a pregnant mother with however much tranquility as could reasonably be expected. At that point both mother and hatchling will be washed in endorphins, the body's "happiness" neurochemicals and common painkillers. Contemplation, giggling, work out, and being in nature all lift endorphin levels. I suggest that moms utilize the accompanying contemplation every day during and after pregnancy to harvest the tranquil otherworldly, passionate, and physical advantages of endorphins.

INSURANCE STRATEGY

A Meditation for Mothers: Feeling the Goddess Within

Take five minutes to inhale gradually and profoundly. Put your hand on your heart and flood yourself with affection and gratefulness for who you are as a mother. Experience the gift, the appreciation, the glow, and the association of being a parent. Moms are goddesses of creation. Maternal supporting is a demonstration of profound love. Feel the intensity of the mother goddess profound inside you. She is the piece of you that is associated with the earth and every common cycle in a significantly mysterious manner. The mother goddess was revered by different societies in antiquated occasions. Lift up in the mother goddess inside you. Feel her base power, and hail her quality in your being.

Your baby responds as you respond, so having a positive perspective is significant. Keep your child quiet by being quiet yourself. Think hopeful and serene contemplations. Additionally, move your body without any difficulty. The delicate influencing your hatchling encounters when you go for a moderate stroll puts you both in a soothing state, Also, after birth, shaking movements help your infant to rest.

Empath moms must be caring to themselves during pregnancy since feeling another being inside can increase their sensitivities. To adjust to your infant, place your hand over your gut, affectionately stroke it, and send your youngster heart vitality. Your accomplice can do this with you as well. It's a method for vigorously saying "hello there" and building up a sweet bond among guardians and kid. Any tension you may have felt about being pregnant can disseminate when you naturally tune in. One empath mother imparted this to me: "I could feel the developing hatchling. My little girl loosened up her wings in all sides of my paunch like a butterfly. I knew it all was alright."

Empath fathers must conform to another degree of affectability during the pregnancy as well. One dad who is a physical empath revealed to me he encountered his better half's morning ailment, even before she knew about it. On an oblivious level, he instinctively converged with her body and felt her sensations. He was better ready to draw a limit between his significant other's vitality and his own in the wake of learning contemplation and establishing practices in our sessions. Utilizing these techniques, he was then less inclined to take on her side effects.

When your infant is conceived, on the off chance that you presume your kid is an empath, take additional consideration to make a satisfying and serene condition, with delicate lighting and negligible clamor. Breastfeeding will develop your holding, just as conveying your child in a sling, which enables both of you to feel the closeness of your energies. This is a great deal more supporting than placing an infant in a bunk with a pacifier or a jug at whatever point they cry.

The Effect of Early Trauma on an Adult's Sensitivity

As a specialist, I've seen how youth disregard or abuse can influence the affectability level of grown-ups. Various empaths I've worked with have encountered early youth passionate or physical injury, which wore out their guards and made them increasingly touchy for the duration of their lives.

An irate domain can particularly affect a touchy kid. As of late, analysts at the University of Oregon found that babies become unsettled around factious and furious voices and that progressing introduction to contentions can make them increasingly responsive to different sorts of pressure and rest disturbances.6 Parents must understand the impact of outrage and hollering on their infant. They should figure out how to quiet themselves and address outrage in more advantageous manners. Babies are absolutely needy. They can't leave your outrage and should endure the dangerous outcomes. The examination likewise uncovered that desperate stressors of misuse and abuse can essentially modify a child's mental health— a calming eye-opener.

I suggest that all empaths who have encountered careless or harsh child rearing find support from an advisor or other qualified manual for recuperate these injuries. I likewise recommend rehashing a variety of the Serenity Prayer to discharge the past, just as any desire that your folks will change. Saying this supplication can shield you from harboring dangerous feelings of disdain and agony from your childhood. It will assist you with discovering acknowledgment just as more harmony and amusingness, regardless of how restricted your folks were. The less feelings of hatred we hold, particularly about our family, the better it is for us and our very own kids.

Furthermore, it's likewise mending and essential to pardon yourself for your very own slip-ups as a parent with your children and family. Try not to pummel yourself. It's difficult to be great, however it's a decent practice to rapidly present appropriate reparations to your friends and family when you've been, state, anxious, disappointed, or peevish. As you offer some kind of reparation, I propose that you affectionately take a gander at your youngsters or accomplice and rehash the delicate customary Hawaiian Ho'oponopono supplication (to one side).

Saying this petition makes positive vitality while it gets out hatred and hurt emotions. It strengthens the extraordinary otherworldly exercises of child rearing, which incorporate self esteem, quietude, and the pledge to respect your own, your children's, and your accomplice's sensitivities.

Twenty Tips for Nurturing Empathic Children

It's superb to help delicate youngsters and grasp their capacities. This will have a significant effect in their inclination OK with themselves now and as they develop into delicate grown-ups. The accompanying procedures can support you and them:

1. Energize your kid's sensitivities and instinct. Welcome your youngster to talk straightforwardly about their capacities to you and to other people who are steady. Make it obvious to them that not every person is tolerating of these blessings and recognize

individuals who may be sheltered. You can likewise share a portion of your empathic encounters, for example, the inclination to take on others' feelings and stress, in spite of the fact that I wouldn't overshare agonizing subtleties. The fact of the matter is to be there for your kid, not treatment for yourself. Show your youngster to esteem their uniqueness and to confide in their hunches and inward voice. At that point they will consider their to be as common. These discussions will enable your kid to feel seen and better comprehend their own responses.

2. Respect your youngster's emotions. Listen cautiously to what your youngster feels, and regard their emotions. This may mean permitting them the periodic day away from work from school to slow down or giving them a chance to play alone more regularly. You would prefer not to enjoy confinement, however you would like to help the required time alone that is basic for an empath youngster's prosperity. On the off chance that your youngster needs to slither under the lounge area table or leave a huge social event, don't drag them once again into the gathering. Try not to disgrace them for needing to get away. Simply let them remain uninvolved where they can watch and ingest without turning out to be overpowered. They are taking an interest, yet in their own specific manner. You might be astonished at the experiences they share after the group scatters.

3. Instruct relatives and instructors about your empath kid. Try not to enable others to pass judgment or censure your kid, for example, revealing to them that they have to "toughen up" in light of the fact that they become effectively harmed or upset. Relatives and others may not intend to be rude. They simply need to see increasingly about your kid's touchy personality. Since the school condition can be cruel and unsupportive of empaths, instruct your youngster's instructors about their blessings and their propensity for tangible over-burden. Additionally, request that they bolster your kid in the event that they are being tormented or prodded at school.

4. Trust your instinct. Continue checking out your very own instinct about what your kid needs. Try not to re-think your internal voice or give others a chance to work you out of what it is letting you know. Give your instinct a chance to manage you in bringing up your kid.

5. Help your kid perceive when they've retained others' feelings. Disclose to your child or little girl that delicate youngsters can without much of a stretch be influenced by the feelings of the individuals around them, maybe more so than different children. You may reveal to them it resembles having the option to feel a raincloud or daylight over somebody's head that no one else can see. You can show them an image of Joe Btfsplk, the celebrated funny cartoon character in

Li'l Abner, who consistently has a foreboding shadow drifting over him. He has good intentions however carries incident to people around him.

Empath youngsters can detect the constructive and adverse vibes that individuals transmit. So when you see an abrupt and unexplainable move in your youngster's state of mind or vitality level, disclose to them it's presumable they're getting someone else's feelings. On the off chance that the experience feels better, that is fine, obviously, however in the event that it's awkward or tiring, bolster your kid in getting some separation and converse with them about the experience. When your youngster figures out how to recognize which feelings are theirs and which have a place with another, they will be less confounded.

6. Be a passionate stabilizer. Empath kids will in general take on their folks' tension and need to improve things for them. Attempt to remain consistent in your feelings and abstain from communicating over the top tension around them. One mother let me know, "In case I'm restless, my delicate child feels it, which destabilizes him and triggers fits of rage. I will likely remain focused. At the point when I'm focused, it makes him have a sense of safety." Be mindful that exceptionally empathic youngsters can reflect your feelings and side effects—and that empath guardians can do likewise with their children.

7. Try not to contend before your kid or anyplace they can catch. Delicate youngsters feel they must assistance their folks show signs of improvement. They become more alarmed and ingest more outrage than kids who are not empaths do. Tension and contentions overstimulate them. On the off chance that you should contend with your accomplice or others, do so when your children can't hear. Like profoundly delicate grown-ups, exceptionally touchy youngsters can be injured by shouting. They may accept they are to be faulted for the contention. They additionally assimilate the cynicism and need to fix the issue, which is an unseemly job for them.

8. Urge your kid to require some serious energy alone to be tranquil and imaginative. Empath kids flourish with free and unstructured time. It's an open door for them to be innovative and enable their minds to meander. They revive and quiet down when they are distant from everyone else, which lessens their incitement limit. Bolster your kid in having these mysterious calm intermissions to renew. You can do this by not overscheduling your kid and by giving them authorization to have normal breaks, particularly when they're grumpy, whiny, or overpowered.

9. Instruct your youngster breathing and reflection works out. At the point when delicate youngsters are focused or feel as though they've taken on others' feelings (counting your own), it's significant that they

figure out how to take a couple of full breaths to quiet down. What's more, they can close their eyes for two or three minutes and picture a loosening up picture, for example, the sea, a cute pet, or a glad day at the recreation center. Request that they center around this picture as they inhale out all inconvenience and breathe in quiet and satisfaction. This will show them how to break the cycle of tactile over-burden and re-focus themselves.

10. Urge your youngster to express their fantasies. Empath youngsters regularly love to share their night dreams. Make a morning meal custom where they can discuss them in detail. Talk about how the fantasy made them feel, what feelings came up, and what message they think the fantasy was conveying. For example, if your kid is disappointed in a fantasy, attempt to recognize a wellspring of the dissatisfaction in day by day life as well with the goal that it tends to be assuaged. You may propose that they keep a fantasy diary where they record their fantasies every night. They can likewise draw or paint pictures from their fantasies in the diary.

11. Help your youngster work on protecting around vitality vampires. Urge your youngster to perceive depleting and upsetting individuals and to define sound limits with them, regardless of whether these individuals are grown-ups or different children. For example, your kid can restrain the time they go

through with a drainer by saying, "I need to go meet my mother now," and they can just avoid irate individuals to forestall getting dumped on. On the off chance that they can't maintain a strategic distance from the individual, show your youngster to picture a defensive shield of white light a couple of inches from their skin that totally encompasses their body from head to toe. Clarify that this shield will repulse negative vitality with the goal that they don't take on awkward sentiments, while the shield will likewise enable positive vitality to come through.

12. Ground your youngster with drumming. Drumming is a base sound that can quiet kids. At the point when your delicate kid gets overstimulated or crotchety, have a fabulous time together pulsating on a drum in a gradual musicality that emulates the pulse. Shaking a clatter can likewise help ease pressure. At the point when your youngster is more seasoned, you can join a drumming circle with your locale—as long as the gathering isn't excessively enormous.

13. Diminish presentation to animating circumstances. Since empath youngsters can get peevish from an excessive amount of tangible info, limit your kid's time in profoundly invigorating conditions, for example, Disneyland and other entertainment meccas. A few hours might be the most extreme time for them, in spite of the fact that others in your gathering can endure more. It's no fun hauling around a shouting kid

when you're at "the most joyful spot on earth." So go early, when the groups are more slender. At that point enjoy a reprieve when you see indications of overburden and come back to your lodging or home. You can generally return for all the more later, after everybody has gotten an opportunity to invigorate and re-focus themselves.

14. Make vacation before your kid rests. This implies no TV, mobile phones, web-based social networking, computer games, PCs, or other electronic gadgets before bed. It regularly takes an empath youngster longer to slow down around evening time. Haziness and calm reduction incitement, which enables youngsters to rest all the more adequately. Singing children's songs relieves them to rest also.

15. Breaking point your youngster's admission of handled nourishment, starches, and sugar. This will bring down your youngster's incitement level by anticipating the emotional episodes from sugar rushes just as starch longings and surges. Handled nourishments are brimming with synthetic compounds and deprived of supplements, which likewise makes them less edible. They can make your children be bad tempered, have excessively or too little vitality, and obscure their core interest. Touchy kids are delicate to nourishments. Teach them about how what they eat impacts their state of mind and vitality level.

16. Intercede before fits. In the event that your youngster is disturbed or very nearly a fit of rage, diminish the lights to mollify nature and turn on loosening up music—no hard rock, substantial metal, or rap. Here and there it's useful to play nature sounds, for example, streaming water. Likewise request that your youngster delayed down and take some long, full breaths. Instruct them to breathe out pressure and to breathe in serenity.

17. Use fragrance based treatment with basic oils (no synthetics). Lavender is unwinding. Rub one to two drops on your kid's third eye (in the focal point of the brow), or warmth lavender oil with the goal that the aroma pervades the room (you can generally get the gadget that securely warms fundamental oils any place you buy the oil). Cleaning up at sleep time with a couple of drops of lavender, chamomile, sandalwood, or ylang oil in the water can be quieting. Advise your youngster to envision washing endlessly all worry in the shower. Including a large portion of a cup of Epsom salts is helpful for evacuating poisons and diminishing worry also. A back rub during or after the night shower can calm your kid and energize rest as well.

18. Utilize pet treatment. Pets are establishing and offer youngsters unqualified love. They are great buddies and can calm an annoyed kid. Empath youngsters have an extraordinary fondness for

creatures and might have the option to speak with them on profound levels in the event that they are creature empaths. Canines can be compelling in settling down overactive or forceful children.

19. Use gemstones. Have a go at giving your youngster a quartz or pink or dark tourmaline precious stone to hold. These can have a sense of safety in the hand, while they unpretentiously are establishing and quieting.

20. Help your kid turn the dial down on pressure. Alongside the above tips, you can likewise show your kid to utilize the accompanying perception to calm down and break the pressure cycle at whatever point they're feeling over-burden. They can utilize it at home, at school, or with their companions. This method is a piece of the fundamental toolbox for every delicate kid.

INSURANCE STRATEGY FOR SENSITIVE CHILDREN

Turn the Dial Down on Stress

At the point when your kid feels overstimulated, this is what you can say to them: In your creative mind, picture a major dial on a table before you. It has numbers on it, and they go from 10 on the left side to zero on the correct side. As of now, this dial is set at ten. See yourself gradually turning the setting on the dial down, beginning with 10. Turn the dial clockwise to one side, as the numbers get littler and littler, until you arrive at zero: 10, 9, 8, 7, 6, 5, 4, 3, 2, and 1. As you turn the dial along these lines, feel yourself getting increasingly loose. You are bringing down your pressure and distress. At the point when you arrive at zero, you will feel quiet and glad.

In the event that your kid is too youthful to even think about imagining this dial, you can draw an image of it and have them point to their anxiety. At that point gradually tally down with them until you arrive at zero.

The down to earth techniques I present in this part will make bringing up an empathic youngster a more quiet and progressively blissful experience for your entire family. It is a gift to help the unique blessings of empath youngsters. At the point when they figure out how to deal with their sensitivities right off the bat, their adolescence and grown-up lives will be simpler and all the more satisfying. From this point of view, we're reminded that child rearing is a sacrosanct duty.

The future of enlightened parenting

My fantasy is that instruction about being an empathic kid starts at the most punctual stages for guardians, just as for instructors in our schools. Rather than disgracing kids for their sensitivities, guardians, instructors, and authority figures can bolster these capacities and help empathic youngsters and their friends and family get them. Along these lines, youngsters will figure out how to comprehend and adapt to their sensitivities also, which can touch off their inventiveness and certainty.

Together we can start to grasp delicate youngsters and grown-ups. The world would be increasingly amicable and tranquil if our pioneers were profoundly touchy individuals with enormous, solid hearts. Through my workshops, books, online courses, and sound projects, I have committed my profession to teaching the same number of individuals as I can—remembering pioneers for all fields and organizations, just as healers and guardians—about empaths and child rearing delicate youngsters. Envision the magnificent day when we all can be available to the miracles of the sensitivities in our youngsters and ourselves.

Chapter 11: Clairvoyant Healing

If you've decided to awaken and strengthen your psychic abilities, you are probably in tune with your compassionate side. If you're like most psychics and want to use your gift to help people, you can use clairvoyant healing – also known as psychic healing – as well as giving them psychic readings. People who have a desire to become psychics or have a natural predisposition to psychic ability are naturally compassionate and empathetic people, so it's no wonder that a great many of them decide to become healers and help others. This may be something you wish to pursue, or perhaps not – but either way, this chapter will cover the basics of psychic healing so that you can begin helping others.

What you're doing when you're healing someone using your psychic power is sending them and their body healing energies. You're basically balancing and harmonizing their body's energies and removing blockages to dissipate physical aches and pains. It's a system of energy work where you are sending specific healing energy to the person who needs it. Clairvoyance comes into play because clairvoyant premonitions often help psychics by showing them images of the problem that can help them come to the solution of how to go about healing them. Psychic healers will also send someone clairvoyant healing images to manifest their "patient" as healthy, happy, and mentally, physically, and spiritually well.

To start healing someone, it can be helpful to meditate. You may even be visited by that person's spirit guide, giving you advice on what the problem is and how to handle it. Whether you've received a clairvoyant premonition, or you were told by them or their spirit guide what they need specific healing for, focus on your subject. It is best if the person you are healing is in the room with you, especially when you're first starting this healing journey. Clear your mind of anything except what you are trying to heal. With every inhale, you are drawing the unhealthiness out of that person's body, with every exhale, you are releasing it into the universe to be transformed into something positive. Draw on the Universal Energy as a source of power to help heal this person, as this can be a very energy depleting process if you work unaided. Visualize images of health. Imagine that they are the image of perfect health, from their head down to their toes. Start from the head, picturing them smiling and relaxed, breathing naturally, a glow radiating from them. Work your way slowly down the body picturing each body part in perfect working condition, even if that part is already healthy. The body must work as a whole – strong arms, heart beating steady, smooth skin, and sturdy legs that can carry them as far as they need to go in life. Keep picturing each part all the way to the feet. Imagine the area that's troubling them as a dark spot on their body. Dissolve it with your energy, watch it dissolve and fade away with pure light, leaving a radiant white glow behind. Then release and send this image of health via energy and clairvoyance to the person you are healing. They may not be able to see them consciously, but the energy and focus you put into them of healthiness will merge with their energy and their mind, showing their subconscious what they are working towards. It will manifest itself as you have also sent it out to the universe.

It is theorized that physical ailments can all be traced back to mental turmoil. Of course, if an outside factor has a hand in things, then this would not be the case. For example, a broken leg is not due to depression; it's due to your subject tripping or falling and the bone breaking. 24-hour nausea directly after eating at a two-star restaurant is probably not because of an inner battle with stress over a work decision – more likely it is food poisoning and nothing deeper is going on in these cases. However, with things like headaches, joint stiffness, muscle pain, intestinal problems, frequent nausea, etc., it is always worth examining a person's mental state. Is there a lot of built up repressed emotion? Depression? Worries and anxiety? Stress due to day-to-day problems or big decisions and events coming up in a person's life? These can all show themselves in physical ways as persistent ailments in the body that just won't go away. Usually, a certain point of physical pain is indicative of energy blockage. So, remember when you're healing, you're not just healing the body; you are also healing the mind. It's always worth it to consider the mental state.

There is no person alive who has suffered nothing and has no emotional issues that cause hindrances in their life. Every single person has been through hard times – although some more than others – but it doesn't invalidate the lasting effects it can have on the mind. When doing mental healing, keep in mind that everyone's been through different things and are dealing with different things in their current life, so don't treat every healing session the same, just as you wouldn't heal a headache the same as a sore stomach. Ask the person you are healing to look into their mind. What is or has been their mental state recently? If they don't want to tell you then that's fine, just have them acknowledge and be aware of anything that comes up and feel the energy of it. As this occurs, you may begin to pick up on a shift in energy. The psychic healer's job is to heal those physical ailments that have an emotional or mental origin. Focus your clairvoyant image messages on what the person is feeling now. Did you sense sadness or depression? Send to them visualizations of them happy and surrounded by a warm glow, perhaps running through a field of yellow flowers. Did you pick up on anxiety or worries? Imagine them completely at peace, eyes closed, face and body relaxed, breathing calm. Maybe they are in a mountain cabin with a cup of tea, nothing but nature around them. Tension and stress? Imagine them going through their hectic day-to-day routine with light ease, the chaos of their duties not phasing them. They are laughing and smiling and almost gliding or floating as they go through their day, light as air. These clairvoyant images will help their subconscious to release and let go of tensions that have been weighing them down and thus will help with whatever the physical symptoms they're experiencing are.

When you have finished a healing session, ask the person you were healing how they felt afterward. Did they feel relaxed? Did a peace of mind come over them? Any bodily sensations? Did any emotions come up for them? How about energy levels? Do they feel like they have more energy, less energy, or the same? Get feedback from this person and follow up a few days after the session to see if any improvements have come up or remain. If it was a specific physical ailment you were treating, ask how it felt immediately after the session and then follow up a few days later to see if your healing had an effect on it, if there was any improvement, and if it's lasted. Remember, you may not have a great effect right away. And if someone improves but it doesn't stick, remember it may take a few sessions – it usually can't just be done in one.

When you are psychically healing someone, be aware that it may take multiple sessions, especially if it's something more serious. However, as a beginner, it's best if you work with smaller less serious ailments to practice. You also have to note that the person you are healing has to want to be healed for your energy to have an effect. They may even say they want to be healed, but deep down, they don't want to be, or they are skeptical. If that is the case, then they will be a struggle to heal, and it may have no effect at all. Just make sure that you don't accuse your very first "patients" of not wanting to be healed because this may be due to your beginner status and inexperienced powers rather than their disbelief or subconscious unwillingness.

You can also clairvoyantly heal someone who isn't near you. In fact, they could be quite far away. This is described by many as praying. What you are doing is the same as if the person was in the room with you; you are sending them energy and clairvoyant images to heal. Try healing from a distance once you've practiced and built up your power healing someone in physical proximity to you. Since they won't be with you physically and you can't feel their energy present, you will have to visualize them more vividly and strongly. Picture every detail of them, and really put a lot of depth, detail and focus into the image of them as healthy and healed. Visualization is the key to distance healing since you don't have their energy to work with. You can even speak what you want for them out loud. The energy of your words will be released into the universe and solidified, manifesting these results of health for your friend or person whom you're trying to heal. Remember: when psychic healing, if you only rely on your own energy reserves, you will become drained quickly. Tap into the universe's energy; it will be an invaluable source of aid during your healing session.

If you want a test subject who won't demand results and won't complain or be skeptical, try with your pet. Maybe they aren't in need of healing but try sensing their energy, and through meditation, focus on your pet and specifically the health of your pet and see if any clairvoyant messages show up. If not, it's still a good way to practice getting a sense of someone else's energy and emotional state, as animals feel things just like we do.

Hopefully, this chapter has awakened you and opened your eyes to the source of many people's physical troubles. Whether you want to become a clairvoyant healer or not is of no importance. Not all psychics choose this path, though they may dabble in it. And choosing this path does not mean giving up every other aspect of psychic ability. It is just one ability that a psychic can develop. If this interests you, practice, practice, and practice – and don't forget to get permission from a friend, partner, or family member to practice your healing on them. Probably best to practice on someone who *has* some sort of physical ailment. Happy healing!

One last note for this chapter: it is extremely important that you are aware that psychic healing is not a cure. You CANNOT make diagnoses through clairvoyant psychic healing. Leave diagnosing patients to the professionals! It is highly unlikely that psychic healing will cure physical ailments completely or can be substituted medicine for illness and pain or medication and therapy for someone with a mental disorder. It can alleviate symptoms, get to the root of problems, get energy flowing and balanced again, and bring up someone's energetic frequency, but it should not be used instead of modern medicine or as a replacement for it. Rather, it should be used alongside it – they can work together.

Chapter 12: Telepathy

Have you ever watched a movie where two people communicate just with their minds or where someone reads another person's thoughts to gain information? Have you ever wished you could do that? Telepathy (from the Greek "tele" meaning "far away" and "patheia" meaning "to be affected by") is communication between minds – but like all aspects of psychic ability, it's not exactly how it's depicted in the movies. However, it is possible to practice telepathy in real life; it's just subtler. You may have even done so without meaning to – for example, if you've ever been thinking about someone or really wishing to hear from someone, and soon after they call or text out of nowhere with no previous planning. This is a form of telepathic communication. The two of your minds were communicating without knowing it, causing the person who called you to make the decision to call – or maybe their decision to call is what brought them into your mind and got you thinking about them. It's no coincidence when things like this happen. There are always psychic channels at work in situations such as these, and like psychic premonitions, everyone has the ability to use telepathy; it's just an area in our mind that needs to be exercised but that most of us ignore or don't believe in due to how we were raised, the society or religion we were brought up in, etc.

When using telepathy, it may not be possible to carry out a full conversation with your BFF using just your minds, but you can transmit images, words, or feelings to one another. To start, let your friend know that you want to try communicating with them telepathically. This is important especially when you're beginning because you will both need to be in a relaxed, focused and receptive state. You can try meditating or deep breathing before to prepare so that your body and mind are relaxed. They don't have to be in the same room or space as you; they can be at their house or even in another town. Close your eyes and try to tune out any background noise or distractions, and really focus your thoughts on your friend. Visualize them clearly in your mind's eye – their essence, their presence, details of their physical features. Once you have solidified this visualization of them as if they are almost there with you, visualize the word, image or feeling you want to send to them. Solidify it, make it vivid in your mind's eye. Make it your mind's only focus. Now visualize your friend, and visualize communicating this image to your friend. Imagine them receiving your message. They should have their mind open and receptive to your message at this point, and they should be visualizing you in their mind's eye. Once you've done this, relax, and let your message drift to the other person. Let it drift from your mind. At this time, you can relax your energy and focus. When the exercise is complete, follow up with them and ask them what they thought or saw in their mind's eye. Make sure to clarify that they shouldn't force any messages; they should just let their mind flow where it will and keep track of what may pop up.

Don't get discouraged if it doesn't work right away. It will take practice and possibly many tries. This is just one way to begin practicing, but no matter how you practice or whom you practice with, stay relaxed (both physically and mentally) and keep your mind open and receptive for both sending and receiving messages.

It's important to be in an environment that is totally comfortable, familiar and relaxing to you, to avoid the risk of distraction or being snapped out of your focus by strange noises, people, smells, etc. When you are just beginning your telepathy journey, and you've just started to practice, the best place to start is in your own home, maybe your bedroom or a room you find particularly relaxing. If your house is hectic and chaotic or you just can't feel relaxed there, try your backyard or a quiet park somewhere in a natural setting. Nature can help ground you and energize your powers. As long as it's a place you can tune out effectively, it should work.

The other commonly known aspect of telepathy is reading the minds of others. Telepathy is harder to practice on strangers, so again first practice with someone you are close with – a willing friend, family member, or partner. When attempting to read their mind, make sure to ask permission. Mind reading won't reveal to you a play by play of what they are thinking, but it will give you a vague idea, sense, or maybe a word or image related to what they are thinking about. Again, the same as with telepathic communication, you want to be in a setting that relaxes you. Close your eyes, tune everything out, and focus your energy on the person whose mind you are trying to read. Get the other person to picture something simple like a banana, and really focus on it. Obviously, they can't tell you what they are thinking. Once they confirm they have solidified their image, visualize them, try and connect with their energy, and let your mind flow. They do not necessarily have to connect with you or be on the same energy level for this practice because, as opposed to if they were sharing their image with you via telepathic communication, mind reading is more of a one-way street/one-man job. Make a note of all the things that flowed easily – not forced – through your mind and check in with them to see if you got anything right. Say, for instance, you saw the color yellow, or smelled banana bread, or felt disgusted (maybe they hate bananas). Don't be discouraged if you didn't get anything right the first few times you try this.

An additional way to practice with someone you know is to prepare yourself accordingly but then ask them a question out loud. Tell them not to answer it but just think about and process how they feel about it and what they would answer to it. It can't be a question you know or suspect the answer to. Right after you ask it, they will likely have an immediate reaction and/or thought, so assuming you're relaxed and your mind is receptive, see what enters your mind immediately after asking the question. Check in with them to see if you accurately picked up on anything.

Once you've built up from these exercises and think you are ready for a challenge, try mind reading next time you're on public transit or in a crowd somewhere. Do this as unobtrusively as you can. If you sense that someone's energy is really blocking you out and doesn't want to let anyone in, they want their privacy. Leave them be and try someone else who's perhaps more receptive. One common thing mind readers pick up on when reading minds are people's emotions. It's probably the easiest thing to access using telepathy, and you've probably read people's emotions telepathically before without even knowing it. It's important to distinguish body language and facial cues giving you information on someone, and telepathy providing that information. To remain unbiased and make sure telepathy is your only source of information, try to focus on someone's energy rather than looking at them/their appearance. You may focus on someone, trying to pick something up from them and feel a rush of worry wash over you. You may even pick up the reason why they are worried, though perhaps in a vague sense, and it may take more experience to get this specific.

In a way, mind reading is similar to psychometry, which we touched on in Chapter 2. You are trying to pick things up from a person: thoughts, emotions, images, etc. Except you can get a reading from them without actually touching them, which would be especially weird while practicing on a crowd of strangers in public.

What's important to remember with telepathy is that patience is key. It is not going to click overnight; in fact, it may take quite a while before you effectively get the hang of it, so don't be hard on yourself if you don't find that you are successful right away. You also may feel energetically drained after a session. Don't draw your practice out for too long as telepathy really works out your brain and it may exhaust you. If a message isn't going through, just plan to try it again another day. Don't deplete your mental power. And remember: when practicing either telepathic communication or mind reading, do not look at that person's face directly (if possible), as facial features and movements may cloud your judgment, mental focus, and force the reading or interpretation. Try to do it as best as possible using only your mind, so if you get it right, you can be sure it was telepathy, and there was no bias involved.

Chapter 13: Aura and Aura reading

What are Auras

Most of us have been in a situation in which auras have been casually brought up in the conversation. Many people are left wondering what an aura is and what they mean. This confusion generally stems from a lack of understanding, and with so many different ideas about what an aura is, this is understandable. However, like most anything else, all it takes is a little education to make things much clearer. If you know about auras, the next time it is brought up in conversation you will have some correct information to share. You might also find that a lot of people will be very curious to hear what you have to say. There are many people interested in auras and aura reading than what you may think. There are still skeptics out there which make some people hesitant to ask questions or seek out information on their own.

On a fundamental level, it is the magnetic field surrounding every living thing that makes up an aura. A person's aura is unique and reflects their own particular energy, it is this energy that impacts their capacity to connect and interact with others. Most people's auras extend about three feet around them, but those who have suffered a tragedy or a trauma usually have a larger aura. Much of what we do in our lives leaves some type of mark on our aura, that is why experienced readers are able to tell so much about a person during a reading. Our aura is so intimately connected to both our minds and our bodies, that it is difficult to keep secrets from experienced readers. This is why it is good to choose a reader than you think you can trust and that you feel comfortable with.

The study of chakras is an ancient tradition and was often treated more like a visit to a doctor. It was known that the chakras held information about both our mental and physical health, so it would make sense to see someone about chakra alignment if there was an issue. Our auras originate from these chakras and therefore, can also reveal what ails us. Many people believe that getting regular aura readings keeps them healthy because the aura can reflect some diseases or illnesses before more classic symptoms arise, increasing the likelihood of a speedy and full recovery.

Experienced aura readers do not even need to meet their subject in person in order to give a proper reading, they can just do it from a normal photograph.

That is how deeply connected we are to our auras, they show up in regular photographs, meaning they must be pretty powerful for that to happen. Auras can always change, because they reflect our thoughts and emotions, so while some of the basic traits, both and good and bad remain the same, other aspects of our aura shift along with our moods and circumstances.

An aura is not one single unit like a sheet, instead, it is made up of many different layers. The aura's layers interconnect and mingle that form the cohesive body that is known as the aura. Each layer of the aura holds different types of information, these are known as the subtle bodies. The energy created by the chakras are what create the auras. The size of a person's aura depends on their spiritual, emotional, and physical health, these auric layers will contract or increase depending on these facets.

Aura reading both visually and energetically is a useful skill for the psychic because it helps you get a sense of the person you're doing a reading for – what they're like as a person and what their current emotional and mental state is. You can pick up on any worries or reservations they may have, as well as what mood they're in coming into the reading. Having this knowledge can help you tailor the reading to the subject. As a psychic, you'll find that no two people, and therefore no two readings, will be the same. You may want to use different techniques, tools, and ways of explaining premonitions to someone based on the insights you have picked up from them.

Your aura is your energy field. It is a reflection of yourself and your current state of being. It can be weighed down and get clogged with negative energies, so here's how to cleanse and refresh it.

First, you'll want to imagine your aura. You don't need to necessarily see any particular colors or light in your mind's eye, but just visualize it around you and focus on this knowledge that an energy field surrounds you. You should be relaxed, and your eyes should be closed while doing this. Now, think of what negative interactions or thoughts you may have had or may have been directed towards you recently. Hanging on to these interactions is usually one of the big causes of aura blockage. Let them go. If you have to bring it up to someone and apologize or have an honest conversation with them, then do so. If not, then there is no reason for you to be carrying it with you. Imagine on every exhale you are letting go of a negative thought, worry, or stressor from your mind. Every time you inhale, you are reenergizing and reinvigorating your aura, bringing a renewed feeling to your once cluttered energy field, which is now a blank space again. You obviously can't eliminate everything from your aura; otherwise, there would be no essence of yourself in it anymore. What you're trying to do with this exercise is release all the negative clutter that can build up over time and make you feel dragged down, low in energy and even depressed. Do this exercise a few times to really clear out all the stagnation. You can find your own visualization technique – whatever will work best and be most effective for you. And try and take breaks from the chaos of life and responsibility. Spend extra time in nature or someplace that will make you feel comfortable and at peace.

Your aura may also be stagnant because you are in a stagnant spot in your life. Do some deep digging and introspection to see if you can get to the bottom of this. Is there some aspect of your life that you don't like? Do you feel unfulfilled? Is it time for a change? No amount of deep breathing is going to answer these questions. If you think they are applicable to how you feel, you're going to have to tackle them, no matter how hard it may be. For your own wellbeing, you need to get to the bottom of what aspect of your life needs an adjustment. If you remain stuck energetically like this, it will also hinder your psychic abilities, making you feel too lethargic or low in energy to practice with your gift effectively. Take care of your aura as you would take care of your physical self.

Treat your aura's blockages as you would treat an illness or a broken bone.

Chapter 14: Mediumship

So far, we've talked about psychic reading. In this chapter, we will talk about medium reading. So what's the difference? Well, someone who does psychic readings may not have mediumistic abilities, which are acting as a vessel and a bridge of communication between the spirit world and the world of the living – but all mediums have psychic abilities, as this is what they use to contact the spirits of the dead.

Mediumship or mediums may be a term you haven't heard before. As mentioned above, a medium is a person who is a bridge between the dead and the living. They can communicate with those that have passed over and convey messages to the living for them. If you've ever used a Ouija board, this is one form of mediumship, as you are contacting, or attempting to contact, the spirits of the dead – although Ouija boards are usually used as a form of entertainment more than anything serious.

The forms of mediumship used by practicing mediums are when the spirit of the dead speaks through the medium, and when the medium receives messages clairvoyantly (or clairsentient, claircognizant, clairaudient) and relays the message to the living. Most often the medium is asked by a living person to try and contact and create a channel of communication with a dead loved one because they miss them and/or because there is unfinished business or unanswered questions between them and they want a sense of closure. The spirit of the dead loved one likely feels the same so that these sessions can be very healing.

If you wish to become a medium, an intermediary between the spirit world and the living, you will need to have a strong hold on the four intuitive types (even if you favor one more than the others) as the messages will come through, and you will perceive them via clairvoyance, clairaudience, clairsentience or claircognizance. This is something to try once you've been practicing your psychic abilities for a while and feel confident. You can still be on a beginner's path, but make sure you've got the basics down. If you feel that you are a natural psychic medium, someone who has sensed the presence of spirits of the dead from a young age, then you may already have an idea of how to communicate and use these spirit channels. This is not a necessity to becoming a medium, however.

If you know any mediums, or if you find that there is a local practicing medium you can get in touch with, ask them about their craft. How does it feel to communicate with spirits? When did they start or when did they first notice they had this ability? What are some examples of mediumistic experiences they've had? You can also search online to read first-hand experiences from mediums if there are none you can contact where you live. Just be careful that the person you are learning from is not a scam artist, as the world of psychic practice is rife with frauds looking to exploit people for money.

To begin practice towards contacting spirits, you must be in a state of total relaxation. Find a calm, comfortable spot, without bright lights. Feel the energy of the universe flowing through you, and relax your mind, letting other thoughts that poke at you to fade away. Now it's time to call upon the spirits. Before you do this next step, make sure you've mastered psychic protection against negative spirits and entities as it's possible to accidentally invite a negative spirit into your home (see Chapter 3 for more information). To help reduce the risk of a negative spirit entering your space, think of a specific deceased loved one of yours that you would like to contact (this can also be a pet). That way your call is not extended to any spirit who happens to be around. They are not invited, only your loved one's spirit is. Now call upon them out loud. Ask them into your space and maybe ask a question of them or ask if they have anything to communicate. Call upon them mentally too. Summon up an image of them in your mind, quite detailed, and mentally welcome them into space. If you feel their presence, ask them a question you have prepared beforehand. You may sense them in different ways, whether you smell the cologne they used to wear, hear their laugh or a song they used to sing, see their favorite color or a piece of clothing they used to wear in your mind's eye, or a sudden shift of emotion where you feel warm and full of love. These are just examples to show you that the way you sense them may not be seeing their image speaking to you in your mind's eye. The way they answer the questions may be through images that must be interpreted or through words you see or hear in your mind. If you answer a question and get a strong emotion immediately afterward, this may also be a response. Or if they answer claircognizant, then you will just know the answer. Remember not to force or make up their presence or answers. Just let them flow, and if they don't show up or answer any questions, then that's okay. Just keep reaching out and practicing and stay relaxed. If you pick up nothing, don't force it. Release and try again another time.

You can also try practicing as a medium for a friend, and you can call upon the spirit of their loved one, asking the spirit any questions your friend may have of them. If you really want to challenge yourself, don't ask your friend who the person they want to contact us. Go in blind. Ask them only to picture and think about the person they wish to contact. Keep your mind clear and relaxed, and be open and receptive to any energies and messages you may receive. If images or feelings start popping up, describe them to your friend. You can go online and look up videos of psychics in action to see how this is done. For example, if you're sitting there with an empty mind and all of a sudden, a figure of a man pops into your mind, and then the color red, and then the concept of Thanksgiving dinner, and the smell of cigarettes you would say, "I'm seeing a man, now the color red, and something to do with Thanksgiving. I also smell cigarettes." You obviously will not know what this means, so ask your friend if it has any significance for them. After all, when acting as a medium, the message isn't for you but for the other person, the one the spirit of the dead is connected to. If this is a legitimate message your friend will get it right away, and if they feel like it, they can tell you what it means to them. Maybe the man was their uncle whose favorite color or shirt or car was red, and he always hosted a big family Thanksgiving at his house – it was an annual family tradition. And he smoked which was a familiar and comforting reminder of his presence to all who knew him. This is an example of how a medium reading may progress. You may hear words or phrases from the deceased as well which you should relay to the living person. Tell them everything you see and hear in your message, even if it may not make sense to you, as it may make sense and be important to them. If not, then just keep going. You probably won't get everything right, especially since you are just beginning, so just keep telling them what you are sensing and make sure you aren't forcing these messages. Make sure they are coming to you naturally and clearly from the spirit you have contacted.

Chapter 15: How to Boost Your Psychic Abilities

Although you have psychic potential, you still have to train yourself so that your skills may become finely tuned. The following are some tips to help you enhance your psychic abilities:

Meditate everyday

Meditation allows you to raise your vibration. The spirit energy vibrates at a high frequency. Through meditation, you can heighten your mental and spiritual powers and become capable of performing even greater psychic acts. Meditation is not a resource-intensive activity. You can pull it off almost anywhere. You just require a serene environment and some free time.

Communicate with your spirit guide

Your spirit guide is basically an entity that protects you. They also enlighten you and make you insightful. When you call on their support, you will increase your chances of achieving what you desire. Have a sacred place in which you meet your spirit guide.

Use psychometry

Psychometry is the practice of decoding the energies of an object. If you can become skilled in this discipline, you will receive a tremendous boost to your psychic abilities. Acquire an object that has sentimental value – e.g., a wedding band – and try to envision the energies of the owner.

Flower visualization

To have strong psychic abilities, you have to improve your mind's eye. You can achieve this through flower visualization. The exercise entails picking up a few flowers and holding them in front of you. Now close your eyes and start envisioning each of them separately.

Random visualization

When you are done using the flower to strengthen your mind's eye, you may now explore some randomness. Just close your eyes and lie on your back in a serene environment and invite your spirit guides to show you many great wonders of the universe. Your spirit guides should show you magnificent images and videos.

Take a walk in nature

Psychics feel a tremendous connection with nature. You could take a stroll in a nature park while practicing mindful meditation. Take occasional stops by sweet-smelling flowers and savor their beauty. Lose yourself to the beauty of nature.

Eliminate negativity

You cannot tap into your psychic powers if you harbor tons of negativity. Eliminate your negativity by heightening your self-awareness and being more forgiving to yourself. You also have to take the necessary steps to right the wrongs you have done. Once you're free of negativity, you're in the right headspace to employ your psychic powers.

Believe in yourself

You cannot become a skilled clairvoyant unless you have tremendous belief in yourself. One of the ways of increasing your self-belief is through reading about those before you who have succeeded. Find books written by successful clairvoyants and read about them so that you can become familiar with their stories. Learn their tricks. The more you study about successful clairvoyants, the higher your odds of becoming successful yourself.

Rest

Quality rest is absolutely necessary. The more you rest, the more energy you have to channel into your psychic activities. One of the best ways to ensure quality rest is by getting enough sleep. You should get at least six hours of sleep every night. This will ensure that your mind is well rested and you're in top physical condition. Having enough rest is crucial for the development of your clairvoyant skills.

Try to read other people's thoughts

This is a perfect way of strengthening your clairvoyant abilities. When you encounter someone, just gaze into their eyes and try to imagine what they are thinking about. If you can accurately read people's minds, then you can rest assured that your psychic abilities are very well developed.

Keep track of your dreams

People with psychic abilities tend to dream a lot. After each dream, ensure you have noted it down on a journal. This will help you keep track of the dreams that came true. When you realize that your dreams are starting to become true, it indicates that your clairvoyant abilities are getting fine-tuned.

Improve your remote-viewing capability

Remote-viewing is the ability to view a place or an event through your mind's eye without you being physically present. To improve your ability of remote-viewing, you have to make good use of your imagination. Start with viewing places near you, and when you get them right, you can move on to far-flung places and objects.

Overcome your fears

If you have any fear in your mind, you will not achieve your full potential as a clairvoyant. You have to eliminate the fear to be able to channel all your mental energies in your psychic activities. The first step toward eliminating fear is to increase your knowledge. The more you know about a situation, the less ignorant you are and the more power and courage you acquire.

Resolve your differences with those around you

If you have problems with other people, ensure that you resolve them. You cannot achieve your full clairvoyant potential when you are not at peace with yourself or other people. Cast away the burden of bitterness and resolve your differences with those around you. This way, your mind is in a position to channel its energies into psychic activities.

Practice seeing auras

This is another great exercise for improving your psychic abilities. Have your friend stand next to a plain-colored wall. Then, look at them using your third eye. Notice if you get to see their auric field. If they have a high vibration, their aura will appear bright.

Ask a friend to call you

Contact your friend telepathically and ask them to give you a call. The more mental energy you invest in this activity, the more likely your friend will call you.

If an empath developed their psychic potential, they could end up becoming so skilled that a career along that line would be in order.

Chapter 16: How to Embrace Being an Empath

Living as an empowered empath is the main goal as you want to be able to use your gifts to their fullest for the betterment of yourself and those around you. You will have to develop a daily routine in order to maintain your level of empowerment. The first key to this success is to stop any negative self-talk. You want to get to a point where you are content with who you are and what your unique gifts bring to the table.

There are many ways to live as an empowered empath; however, here are the top ten steps on getting to that point:

1. You have to love yourself.
2. Take notice of your accomplishments.
3. Make time to be alone.
4. Maintain a healthy diet.
5. Use crystals as well as meditation.
6. Learn how to set and enforce boundaries.
7. Focus on practicing self-awareness.
8. Stay away from toxic people.
9. Create clear goals.

10. Establish a routine.

You have to love yourself. It is important that you have to find a way to love yourself. No more negative self-talk. Follow your gut instead of listening to others. Do not take on other people's emotions, and surround yourself with those that support and love you for who you are. Make a list of the attributes that you love about yourself and remind yourself daily. If you are feeling down, make a point to turn a negative into a positive. If you do not love yourself, it will be difficult to live an empowered life. If you ever doubt yourself, doubt what you are doing with your life, take note of what you have already accomplished.

Take notice of your accomplishments. If you have had any accomplishment in your life, write it down. Take note of even the smallest accomplishments. For instance, when you were in a bout of depression two months ago, you were able to get out of bed and clean your house. This may seem small, but if you find yourself getting back in that place, you will see that you have already climbed out of that space before, and you can do it again. Other accomplishments could include graduating from college, purchasing a new home, getting the new job you have been searching for, and rescuing four dogs. When you are able to recognize what you have accomplished in your life, you are more likely to feel empowered from it and for your future.

Make time to be alone. We have talked about alone time a few times so far. This is because we need it and actually thoroughly enjoy it. If it makes us happy and refreshed, then spend as much time alone as you need. While we tend to focus on everyone else around us, we need to shut that off at times and focus on ourselves.

Maintain a healthy diet. Food translates into energy itself; therefore, if you do not want a bunch of negative energy festering inside of you, cut down on junk foods. Yes, every now and then will not kill us, but make sure you try to eat plenty of fruits and vegetables to maintain a healthy diet.

Use crystals. Crystals can be a source of clarity and calm when you need to rejuvenate your energy zone. One of the most popular stones for grounding and blocking negative energy is tourmaline.

Learn how to set and enforce boundaries. Boundaries can be difficult to set, especially if it is with a loved one. But we are typically bad at setting boundaries no matter who it is. If you do not learn how to set boundaries, you will end up in pain, drained, and burned out.

Focus on practicing self-awareness. The more you become aware of your own energy, the more you will be able to figure out and decipher between someone else's. If you are ever in a situation where you suddenly feel terrible internally, take a moment to figure out whether that is coming from you or someone else.

Stay away from toxic people. This can be difficult because empaths are typically sought out by master manipulators. It is as if they can sense it. If you are in tune with your body, you will feel when someone just is not right. If you do feel that way, run for the hills.

Create clear goals. Make known to yourself what your purpose in life is. If you enjoy helping others, make it a point to try to make a living out of it. Be honest with yourself and know your limits when you are setting goals for yourself; make them attainable and grow from there.

Establish a routine. Routine will help you maintain a level of stability even if it is just in the morning so you can clear yourself for the rest of the day. A few ideas would be to wake up early to meditate, make a list of items that need to be completed that day, have breakfast, shower, and get to work. Your routine may be different; do what works best for you in order to function throughout the day.

The more in tune you are to making sure the above items are maintained, the more empowered and peaceful your life will be. Make sure to focus on yourself and your awareness in order to protect you from toxic people. Maintain your energy, love yourself, and the rest will fall into place.

How to Become an Assertive Empath

Many empaths were raised in such a way that we subconsciously have the urge to help and please everyone around us. As children, we were most likely given the idea of being a good person if we followed orders from a parent or teacher. If we did not follow those orders, we associate it with a form of punishment, hence how the people-pleasing behaviors came about in order to avoid punishment or letting others down. There is a way to balance being an empath while also being assertive. When you are assertive, you are claiming your views and putting forth the right to do so in a confident manner. Basically, being assertive means that you are speaking up for yourself, you are making your thoughts known, and you effectively speak out about your concerns, wishes, and ideas. When you do this, you want to make sure that you are being considerate of others and respectful of other people's emotions and personal boundaries. There are plenty of kind ways to say, "I appreciate you asking me. However, I am unavailable to help at this time." That way, you are not setting yourself up for even more stress.

The most important way to become more assertive as an empath include the following:

1. Set boundaries.

2. Try not to take things personally.

3. Express feelings by writing in an assertive tone.

4. Maintain and control your own happiness.

5. Focus on how you are presenting yourself.

Set boundaries. Setting boundaries is particularly difficult for empaths. We tend to want to make sure everyone is happy. Thus, if they ask for help, we will fit it in our schedule. When you recognize that you are getting into an unhealthy relationship or notice that you are always trying to save, help, or change people, you have to stop before you are the one that gets hurt. Nine times out of ten, you will be the one to get hurt or used. If those around you understand who you are or respect you, they will not mind when you need time to recharge. They should understand that it means nothing against them. If they are not able to understand, then they are not the type of people that you need to be around in the first place.

Try not to take things personally. If someone happens to ignore you one time, you will be wondering why they are mad at you until either it is addressed or you forget about it. It may have been a misunderstanding. In fact, most instances are not intentional; however, you worry about whether or not someone is mad at you.

Express your feelings by writing in an assertive tone. Writing can be good in many ways, especially if you have been hurt or are holding on to past trauma. If you are assertive in any way, start with it in writing. Write what you want to express and express it how you need to in order to feel better.

Maintain and control your own happiness. It is important not to depend on other people when it comes to what makes you happy. If you do depend on others to make you happy, then you will most likely be disappointed every time.

Focus on how you are presenting yourself. Make sure you focus on how you are portraying yourself. You do not want to be so humble that people recognize that and perceive you as a weak person. For instance, if you use too many emojis, you may be seen as insecure and that you want to be liked.

Being an empath can be a struggle; however, there are ways to reduce the possibilities of being taken advantage of and keep those boundaries in place for your own well-being. One of the most difficult things for an empath to say is the word "no." The fear of confrontation and upsetting anyone else is where this stems from. People do not want to say no, as they do not want to upset or hurt the other person. Even when an empath does say no, they tend to worry about the fact that they did, and it does become stressful and overwhelming. We want to be liked, and we want to help, so we typically say yes to anything and everything in order to keep the peace with those around us, even if it means that we will be run into the ground.

Being assertive is not a bad trait. It can be used as a tool in order to manage your obligations to the point where you are not setting yourself up to be drained. Being assertive is somewhat an art. You have to make sure you maintain a level of consideration and respect for other people's feelings. I may be mistaken with passive-aggressive behavior, but it is distinct because you are focusing on other people's needs as well as your own. Once you master the art of being assertive, you will be able to control your life in a stress-free manner that works for you.

Learning How to Set Boundaries

All empaths cringe when they are told to set boundaries. Most likely, people have told you that a few times, especially if you are seeing a counselor. But you most likely will not enforce or put any boundaries in place until you get hurt when you least expect it. Usually, after a traumatic event, you will then think a bit clearer, and it is at that time that you will actively seek to put boundaries in place to avoid further trauma. The best ways to set boundaries are as follows:

1. Focus on how you feel around certain people.
2. Utilize the word "no."
3. Become comfortable with saying no.
4. If you become overwhelmed, leave the scene.
5. Take time for yourself.
6. Create an imaginary bubble.

Focus on how you feel around certain people. If you are near certain people and they drain the life out of you or you get agitated immediately in their presence, it is best to avoid those people. What you need to do is find which environments make you anxious, tired, drained, or overwhelmed. In these environments, it may not just be that you can recognize the moods of other people, but you look at others conversing and pick up on the vibe of their conversation. If you find yourself dreading situations where certain people will be, do what is best for you and try to avoid it.

Utilize the word "no." Say no to people if you do not have any more energy to give. Do not deplete yourself for anyone because, if the tables were turned, most likely, they would not for you.

Become comfortable with saying no. Saying no and actually becoming comfortable with it are two completely different dinosaurs. Anyone can say no. It is following through and being comfortable with it that can be difficult.

If you become overwhelmed, leave the scene. If you are in any situation where you are picking up bad vibes by someone or multiple people, get out! If you are out in a public place and are extremely overwhelmed by the environment, you should excuse yourself and go to the bathroom or for a short walk to remove yourself from the situation. The last thing you want is to have anxiety hit you when you are in a public space with other people. There is no need for you to sit in a place where you are feeling terrible because of the people around you.

Take time for yourself. This has been said multiple times, and if it is said many times, then it is true. You need to take time to recharge your energy. Do what is best for you, such as walking, yoga, meditation, napping, watching television, or whatever helps you relax. You need to make sure you are taking time for yourself to do what calms you in order to maintain your energy and health.

Create an imaginary bubble. This may sound silly, but if you can imagine that you have a protective shield around you, you may feel a bit more safe than usual.

Act as if nothing will hurt you and that you are in control of yourself and your own choices. Do not let toxic people break through to get to you.

Setting boundaries will only upset those who have been taking advantage of you, so pay attention to who has an issue when you do stick to your guns and focus on protecting yourself. Those are the types of people you will want to watch out for the most!

How to Become an Extroverted Empath

Extroverted empaths do exist, and while rare, they have to battle the balancing act between the two. There are many problems that extroverted empaths go through. A few are the following:

- They desire human connection because they are extroverts, but because they are empaths, the more they interact, the more they drain themselves.

- Due to their extrovert nature, they can understand the feelings of a lot of people simultaneously. But they are empaths as well, so they know the intricate details of many people at the same time.

- They are extroverts, so they love to know about the experiences of other people, but this isn't on a superficial level. They want to know about other people on a deeper level because they are empaths as well.

- People think that, because they are extroverts, they don't need much time alone. However, because they are empaths, they want to be alone sometimes.

The balance between wanting to have human connection and needing to have alone time for health and well-being is definitely a complicated mix. You may go through periods of time when you are craving time out of the house, but there are plenty of times that you crave being at home in your own space. If you have a few good friends, they will understand how you operate after a while, and to them, it is okay because they are true friends. Those who do not understand might need to be explained what goes on with your balancing act. If they still do not understand, it would be right to analyze that relationship.

So how do we deal with this complicated balancing act of being an extrovert and empath? Here are a few ways to assist:

1. Use breathing techniques.

2. Block emotions that do not belong to you.

3. Ground and focus on yourself.

4. Take regular breaks.

5. Be alone but with people.

Use breathing techniques. It is important to become aware of yourself, how you operate, what you are feeling at any given time, and how your body needs to recover. When we practice breathing techniques, it allows us to be more in touch with ourselves and aware of our senses. When you familiarize yourself with this technique, you will be able to recognize when your energy needs rejuvenating.

Block emotions that do not belong to you. The more people you interact with, the more you will absorb their energies. For example, the sadness you have been feeling actually belongs to your neighbor who recently lost their mother. The more you block other people's energies, the better off you will be as you will save your own energy and reduce stress and anxiety. Moreover, this will help you manage your feelings in a healthy way.

Ground and focus on yourself. Grounding is a form of meditation that focuses on your body in relation to the ground. For example, if you are sitting on the floor, you should focus on feeling your body touching the floor. Focusing on this will eliminate all other outside elements. The last thing you want to do is carry around other people's energy. It will leave you drained, exhausted, overwhelmed, and ungrounded. The moment you start to feel this way, you should make sure to center your awareness back to yourself. Then you need to ground and focus on getting back into a peaceful place. When we are able to regain focus on ourselves, we are also able to release the energy from others that we have been carrying around.

Take regular breaks. Relaxing can be good for your mind and body. Having some time to yourself to do what you wish will give your mood an uplift, as well as your energy. Empaths need to take breaks in order to replenish themselves. Replenishing yourself is of the utmost importance, so make sure that you first recognize when you need it, and make time to take a break.

Be alone but with people. While we do love people, we may not always want to interact with them. Most of us do love to people-watch as well, so get yourself to a public place where you do not know anyone, and take in the scenery. When we are in a public place without having to interact with others but observe, it is easier to block out their energies and focus on our own.

Extroverted empaths have the balancing act of craving human connection and feeling drained from connecting. It comes and goes in waves. At times, we want to be near people a lot, and at other times, we need to be alone. The more you are in tune with how your mind and body operate, the more harmonious the balancing act will be.

Chapter 17: Common Myths That Psychic Empaths Should Never Believe

As if being highly sensitive to the energy around you is not already a big responsibility, you will also have to contend with a lot of misconceptions about you. As an empath, you really have a big calling on your hands and you need to understand that not everyone will understand this. You might be labeled as being too emotional or too dramatic. You might even be accused of being one of the energy vampires that you are so keen to eliminate from your life. Understanding the many misconceptions that people have in regard to empaths is the first step towards gently educating those around you. Even if you do not feel like being the myth buster in your circle, you can still learn to differentiate the myths from the facts for your own sake. Knowledge is power and having knowledge about yourself is one of the most powerful things you can do for yourself.

Myth #1: Psychic empaths are extremely self-absorbed and only worry about themselves.

Fact: Psychic empaths often care about others more than they care about themselves.

From the outside looking in, the moodiness and emotional nature of a psychic empath can come across as the disposition of a person who is only concerned with how they are feeling. The truth of the matter is that a psychic empath is more likely to be moody because of the people around them, and not because of their own emotions. It is easy to be judgmental towards a psychic empath because of how they carry themselves. They are often quiet and reserved and will not want to come out to play too often. This might be interpreted to mean that they do not care about interacting with others and only worry about themselves. The truth is that while the empath might want to be a ray of sunshine to everyone else, they often find themselves incapable because of the overwhelming feelings they go through when dealing with different energies given out by others.

Myth #2: Psychic empaths are just mentally ill.

Fact: Being highly sensitive is not a mental illness.

Many empaths make for good listeners and confidants based on their ability to empathize and truly feel for others. Because of this, empaths often find themselves the designated dumping ground for all emotional baggage. When you are burdened with the emotional problems of others, it is easy to become depressed and anxious, which might cause others to assume you are mentally ill. Many times, empaths are just sad because of all the emotional burden that they have to shoulder. This immense sadness may mimic the signs of a person that is going through clinical depression. Yes, there are instances when an empath may be diagnosed with depression, but this is not simply because they are highly sensitive. There are numerous factors that must be present for one to be diagnosed with depression. These factors are not exclusive to an empath. They can affect just about anyone, especially those who are genetically predisposed to the same.

Myth #3: Empaths are psychologically weak

Fact: The moments of "weakness" that empaths exhibit are as a result of all the negative energy that they have to deal with.

What might be normal to a typical non-empath may be extremely difficult to the empath. Take, for instance, holding down an office job. For the person that is not highly sensitive to the energy of other people, an office job is just another opportunity to earn a paycheck and advance in their career. For the empath, an office job means being constantly bombarded by the negative energy from all sides. As such, an empath might struggle to hold down a normal 9 to 5 job, while this is just another workday for everyone else. When this happens, the empath might be accused of being weak, lazy, fussy or just unwilling to try. This could not be further from the truth. Being an empath is hard work. Imagine walking through life everyday while someone carries a huge ball that they hit you with every time you take one step. This is how it feels to be an empath. You are constantly being hit by a big ball of negative energy and you must lift yourself up every time you fall from this hit. After a while, it can be easier to stay on the ground because you have run out of energy to lift yourself up. As an empath, it is important to remember that you are not psychologically frail. Being able to deal with other people's negative energy on a daily basis and showing up in the world even though you know what's coming, takes a whole lot of strength.

Myth #4: Empaths are emotionally volatile

Fact: Being exposed to varying emotional energy can make you more in control of your emotions.

People who believe that empaths are emotionally volatile base their arguments on the fact that empaths are often exposed to various energies, which might interfere with how emotionally stable they are. True, it is common for an empath to be moody, but this does not mean that they are always going to lash out when provoked. Many empaths are often moody when they retreat into themselves to introspect on the emotions that they have picked up. This does not make them a volatile person who is at the mercy of their emotions. It is possible for an empath to be highly stable when it comes to their feelings and those of others. In fact, an empath can easily learn how to be calm and in control regardless of those around them by understanding how to process and shield the energy that surrounds them. Some of the calmest and collected people that exist in this world are actually empaths. They have learned to read people and so nothing really takes them by surprise.

Myth #5: Most empaths are cold and detached from everyone else.

Fact: Detachment is a side effect of being emotionally drained.

Many empaths who come across as detached do not become so because they intended to. It is often as a result of being emotionally abused by people around them. When they cannot take it anymore, an empath may become numb as a way of protecting themselves. It is not correct to assume that an empath is cold and unfeeling simply because they are an empath. Even the most outwardly detached empaths tend to have a light of empathy flickering deep inside of them. Empathy is not something you can switch on and off at will. If you care about other people, you will always care about them regardless of where you go or what you do.

Myth #6: Empaths are often highly dependent on their loved ones.

Fact: Empaths like for positive energy to flow both ways.

When an empath finds a source of positive energy, that source becomes an asset that they can draw their strength from. This is why empaths really thrive when they are deeply and genuinely loved. However, unlike energy vampires, empaths realize the need for the flow of positive energy to be two-sided. They love giving as much as they enjoy taking. You are not likely to find an empath that loves leeching on their loved ones. It is also important to note that empaths are not really dependent on positive energy from other people to survive. They are capable of doing it all on their own, as long as they learn how to protect from negative energy around them. If you are an empath, you do not have to worry about being a leech to others. As long as nobody is complaining, and as long as you can feel the good, positive energy flowing both ways, then it is safe to assume that the people in your life love you and the presence you bring.

Myth #7: Empaths are just glorified doormats.

Fact: With the right boundaries, an empath can care about others without feeling used.

Sure enough, empaths struggle with saying no. Empaths often want to take care of others and struggle with the guilt of feeling as if they are not helpful. It is effortless for an empath to find themselves relegated to the role of a doormat if they have not set the limits and boundaries for other people. This; however, does not mean that all sensitive people are just pushovers that allow anyone and everything in their lives. Empaths who are conscious of their powers and abilities know that it is easy for others to take advantage of them. As such, they often have ways of managing the people in their lives and striking the balance between being helpful and being everyone's doormat.

Myth #8: Empaths are all good people.

Fact: Being highly sensitive does not automatically qualify you for decency.

The question of whether a person is good or bad can only be answered after evaluating the choices that the person makes, and not as a factor of their genetic predisposition. Just because a person has been born as an empath does not mean they will always be a good person. An empath is a human being who is capable of hurting others and even making bad choices based on the prevailing circumstances in their life. While it is true that many empaths are often not manipulative people, it is also true that they are just humans and have the choice to be bad or good just like everyone else.

Myth #9: Empaths take to narcissists like moths to a light.

Fact: The relationship between empaths and narcissists is complex.

It has been said that opposites attract, and this could never be overstated in the case of narcissists and empaths. Empaths are the complete opposite of narcissists, and when these two categories of people meet there are often fireworks. Why is this so? Is it because the empath is keen on healing the narcissist? In many cases, the empath is not even aware that they are dealing with a narcissist. This might seem like a contradiction because after all, empaths are supposed to be intuitive and highly capable of reading other people's energy and intentions. Narcissism is a personality disorder that brings forth individuals who are highly manipulative. At the beginning of a relationship, the narcissist might make it seem as if they are the healer that the empath needs. As such, the empath will gravitate towards the narcissist because they seem kind and decent and loving. The narcissist, on the other hand, will pursue the empath because they love the adoration that the empath is able to give so freely. The narcissist-empath relationship evolves to become a highly toxic relationship where the empath keeps on giving and forgiving, while the narcissist cannot stop taking and creating chaos because that is what they thrive in. There is often never a happy ending when a narcissist and an empath meet and fall in love.

Myth #10: All empaths are introverted.

Fact: Empaths can be introverted, or not.

Empaths do not all come in one size. There are different sides to an empath. Some are introverted, some are extroverted, while some are ambiverts. In all fairness, the extroverted empath is rarer than the introverted empath. However, reliable sightings point to the existence of the paradox that is an empath who is extroverted. Being extroverted is more of a personality trait than anything else. As such, you can be a person that loves to be around people and at the same time be highly capable of tuning into the emotions of those people. An extroverted empath gets to live a very conflicting life in that they want to interact with people but at the same time, they do not want to be overwhelmed by it. This is unlike the case of the introverted empath who could not care much for crowds. If you are an extroverted empath, you will need to be careful about how much you take in from others before wearing yourself down. For every two or so hours spent in a crowd, make sure you take some time to catch your breath and process out the negative energy from your body.

Myth #11: You can quit being an empath.

Fact: Being an empath is a life-long sentence.

Many empaths would love to be able to wake up one day and find that their empathic abilities are all gone. It can be overwhelming to be the resident empath, and sometimes you will feel that you need a break from all the caring. Unfortunately, if you are born an empath there simply is no way out of it. Instead of fighting your power, the best thing you can do for yourself is to learn how to harness it for your own good, and for the good of those around you. For example, you can train yourself to learn how to distinguish your emotions from those of others so that you do not carry emotional loads that do not belong to you. You may not be able to stop being an empath, but you sure can learn how to carry this gift without breaking your back.

Myth #12: Empaths are victims of childhood trauma.

Fact: Trauma is not a prerequisite for empathy.

Some people believe that the only way a person can be as emotional as the empath typically is if that person has gone through some form of childhood trauma. It is wrong to assume that a person who is sensitive towards others and in regard to their own emotions is automatically coming from a place of great suffering. True, there are empaths who have suffered greatly at the hands of those who were supposed to love and protect them. However, it is inaccurate to think that the driving force behind empathy is trauma. Some people are simply born with the ability to be highly sensitive. What happens to them as they grow up is a whole different matter.

Conclusion

You should now feel more comfortable with the idea of psychic phenomena. Maybe you have learned to recognize this ability within yourself, and put it into practice to enrich your life. Have you discovered any abilities you share with your friends? In many cases, it happens that people with similar psychic strengths are drawn to each other, whether they recognize it at the time or not. Now that you know that you have the potential, you can learn more about your gifts and how to benefit from them.

You have now acquired a vocabulary of essential terms and concepts that you can carry forward to explore the different aspects of the metaphysical world, and communicate your interest to friends, teachers, and loved ones. The community of people who are open to psychic influences is immense and covers our whole shared history as humans, and all the territory we occupy. You can find people to speak with and study these influences, everywhere you go.

The study of crystals, gemstones, and their influence on us, presents a rich variety of topics. From the health benefits to the history of the earth, the beauty and symbolism of stones connect us to our oldest and best selves.

Practice the exercises in this book as often as you can. Breathing exercises, visualizations, and meditation can all help improve your health and emotional well-being, independent of the impressions and observations you record. If you'd like to go further, there are many schools of meditation and spiritual health where you can learn about the energy fields of the body, the chakras and the organization of the breath, and the many ways in which the physical and metaphysical worlds are paralleled and linked.

Last, but not least, we hope you have made a decision and a promise to trust yourself more often, listen to what you tell yourself, pay attention to the things you think are important, and value your observations.

© **Spiritual Awakening Academy**

Made in the USA
Monee, IL
08 May 2021